Overcoming Unwanted Intrusive Thoughts

A CBT-Based Guide To Getting Over Frightening, Obsessive, Or Disturbing Thoughts

Sally M. Winston, PsyD
Martin N. Seif, PhD

16pt

Read How You Want
LARGE PRINT BOOKS, BRAILLE & DAISY

Copyright Page from the Original Book

Publisher's Note

This publication is designed to provide accurate and authoritative information in regard to the subject matter covered. It is sold with the understanding that the publisher is not engaged in rendering psychological, financial, legal, or other professional services. If expert assistance or counseling is needed, the services of a competent professional should be sought.

Distributed in Canada by Raincoast Books

Copyright © 2017 by Sally Winston and Martin N. Seif
New Harbinger Publications, Inc.
5674 Shattuck Avenue
Oakland, CA 94609
www.newharbinger.com

Cover design by Amy Shoup

Acquired by Jess O'Brien

Edited by Gretel Hakanson

All Rights Reserved

Library of Congress Cataloging-in-Publication Data on file

TABLE OF CONTENTS

"This important book is essential and mandatory reading for anyone affected by unwanted and intrusive thoughts, and their health providers. The authors crystallize decades of experience into a perfectly clear and readable guide. The solution to this misunderstood problem is in this book."
—**Joseph A. Adams, MD,** medical director at Baltimore Health Systems and Step By Step of Maryland, LLC, and past president at Smoke Free Maryland

"I wish I would have had access to this book twenty years ago! Sally Winston and Martin Seif have put all the pieces of the puzzle together to help people understand and overcome unwanted intrusive thoughts. This is a must-read book, packed with information to help people suffering with anxiety-provoking intrusive thoughts, as well as clinicians who are trying to help them."
—**Kimberly J. Morrow, LCSW,** maintains a private practice in Erie, PA; specializes in the treatment of anxiety and obsessive-compulsive

disorder (OCD); provides training and case consultation for clinicians through www.anxietytraining.com; and is author of *Face It and Feel It*

"It turns out that commonsense approaches to stopping our worries, such as pushing thoughts away, arguing with them, or seeking reassurance, actually feed these worries and help them grow. Sally Winston and Martin Seif—two of the brightest minds in our field—deliver a simple yet powerful two-step process for change."
—**Reid Wilson, PhD,** author of *Stopping the Noise in Your Head*

"Finally, here is an effective, neurologically based clinical approach to dealing with unwanted thoughts (without having to use a rubber band). The authors' clear and distinctive voice should be widely heard by cognitive behavioral therapy (CBT) clinicians, and by those engaged in an ongoing and unrelenting struggle with undesirable ruminations."

—Ronald M. Doctor, PhD, professor emeritus of psychology at California State University, Northridge; author; active researcher; and practicing behavior therapist

"In their book *Overcoming Unwanted Intrusive Thoughts,* Winston and Seif tackle one of the great mysteries of human distress and suffering: the seeming inability to rid our minds of unbidden, unwanted, and disturbing thoughts, images, and memories. Readers are given a rare glimpse into the nature of unwanted intrusive thoughts, as well as their origin and impact on emotional distress. Written in a warm, engaging, yet knowledgeable manner, this book provides new insights for consumers and professionals alike on why common sense fails to soothe the troubled mind. Readers will find practical, research-based guidance on how to subdue unwanted intrusions and overcome their emotional disruption. This book offers much-needed help for those who struggle with the torment of persistent disturbing thoughts."

—David A. Clark, PhD, professor emeritus in the department of psychology at the University of New Brunswick, and coauthor of *The Anxiety and Worry Workbook* and *Cognitive Therapy of Anxiety Disorders* with Aaron T. Beck

"Tens of millions of people have bothersome intrusive thoughts, and most often these thoughts are so unacceptable or embarrassing that many people have trouble telling anyone about them—even their closest family members or friends. At worst, these intrusive thoughts are part of severe problems such as OCD, but we know that almost anybody under stress can occasionally experience intrusive thoughts. Now, at last, a state-of-the-art psychological program written by two of the leading clinicians in the country with years of experience treating this problem is available. The program in this remarkable little book may be sufficient to help you overcome your intrusive thoughts, if therapeutic assistance may be needed, to guide you to the best available resources. I recommend this program very highly as a first step for anybody dealing with this issue."

—David H. Barlow, PhD, ABPP, emeritus professor of psychology and psychiatry, founder, and director emeritus at the Center for Anxiety and Related Disorders at Boston University

"Winston and Seif have done a wonderful job in providing sufferers of obsessive intrusive thoughts with up-to-date and scientifically accurate information about this often crippling problem. This clearly written guide will serve both as a self-help resource, as well as a workbook to be used as an adjunct to psychotherapy."

—Lee Baer, PhD, professor of psychology in the department of psychiatry at Harvard Medical School, and author of *Getting Control* and *The Imp of the Mind*

"An interesting and original account of a little-understood phenomenon—intrusive thoughts."

—Fredric Neuman, MD, director of The Anxiety and Phobia Treatment Center, and author of *Caring, Fighting Fear,* and *Worried Sick?*

"What a great book for people who struggle with intrusive thoughts! Two highly skilled and respected experts in the treatment of chronic anxiety explain how intrusive thoughts work, what they mean and don't mean, why they defy your best efforts at getting rid of them, and most importantly, how to change your relationship with these thoughts so they don't remain a persistent, negative focus. They help the reader understand that intrusive thoughts don't persist despite your best efforts; they persist because of your best efforts at arguing with, struggling against, and seeking to avoid these unwanted thoughts. Their book offers plainspoken instructions with lots of good examples that will help you let go of the guilt, fear, and confusion that so often accompanies intrusive thoughts. This is a must-read for anyone experiencing such thoughts, as well as the professionals who seek to help them."

—David Carbonell, PhD, is a Chicago-based psychologist specializing in treating chronic anxiety for over thirty years, author of *Panic Attacks Workbook* and *The Worry Trick,* and "coach" at www.anxietycoach.com

"Winston and Seif have written an important and much-needed book. It speaks to those who suffer intensely from unwanted intrusive thoughts and, as a result, descend into a world of anxious isolation. The authors lift the sufferer from a frightening darkness into a world of understanding and onto a path to freedom. This is necessary reading for anyone suffering from the tyranny of unwanted thoughts, and it should be required reading for helping professionals."

—Bruce Shapiro, MD, clinical professor of psychiatry at Columbia University College of Physicians and Surgeons

"If you live in fear of thoughts that pop into your head, this is the book for you! Two expert psychologists explain unwanted intrusive thoughts, and show you how to break free from the cycles that strengthen their grip on you. You don't have to suffer because of your thoughts, and Winston and Seif show you the way out of your suffering. The information, strategies, and abundant examples within these pages make this a must-read for anyone trying to make sense of frightening intrusive thoughts, and wanting relief from the distress they cause."

> **—Joan Davidson, PhD,** codirector of the San Francisco Bay Area Center for Cognitive Therapy, and assistant clinical professor in the clinical science program at the University of California, Berkeley

"As humans, we often pride ourselves on our ability to think ourselves out of the distress and difficulties that we encounter. But these authors help us recognize that we aren't in complete control of our thoughts, and help us to approach our thought processes from a more realistic and healthy perspective. They assist us in identifying common myths about our thoughts, and teach us that fighting thoughts is not the answer—it is part of the problem! With the strategies in this book, we learn how to reduce the stress and distress thoughts can trigger, and this takes away the power of those thoughts. The authors present clear explanations of the brain processes underlying intrusive thoughts, but even more importantly, explain why our typical efforts to overcome these thoughts fail. Finally, they provide a detailed guide of what we can do to reduce distress about unwanted thoughts, and to develop a more accepting relationship with the mind."

—Catherine M. Pittman, PhD, HSPP, licensed clinical psychologist, associate professor of psychology at Saint Mary's College Notre Dame, and coauthor of *Rewire Your Anxious Brain*

To Mort, Carla, Maggie, and Molly
—S.W.

To Samantha, Laura, Sam, Clare, Ruta,
and Adam
—M.S.

Introduction

Have you ever stood on the edge of a train platform, minding your own business, and then suddenly, out of the blue, had the brief thought, *I could jump off and die!* Or have you been struck by the passing thought, *Hey, I could push that guy onto the tracks!*

When a room full of people is asked these questions, 90 percent of them will acknowledge they have.

But there is a second set of questions to ask that is much more important, and contains the key to the issues in this book. Do you get upset or worried that your thoughts might actually lead you to do something awful? Or are you plagued by a thought that you might have already done something bad and somehow it slipped past you? Or that the fact that this thought has crossed your mind must mean something important? Or is there a thought that drives you crazy because you just can't manage to get it out of your mind? Do you live in dread that having bizarre, repetitive, repugnant, or unrelenting thoughts means something shameful or terrible about you? Do you hope and pray that these thoughts won't come around again? But they do, and they continue to haunt you. They have become stuck.

These upsetting, distressing, frightening thoughts that enter your mind unbidden are called *unwanted intrusive thoughts.* Sane and good people have them. If you are plagued by thoughts you don't want—thoughts that scare you—and thoughts you can't tell anyone, this book may change your life.

Our first message is that you are not alone. There are millions of people who have thoughts just like yours. Good people have awful thoughts. Violent thoughts come from gentle people. Crazy thoughts occur for people who are not the least bit crazy. You are not the only one who experiences repeating thoughts that just won't leave your mind.

Our best guesstimate is that there are upwards of 6 million people in the United States alone who, at some point in their lives, suffer from unwanted intrusive thoughts. The silence, fear, and shame surrounding the issue increase the suffering and isolation of many good people. You bear your burdens in isolation, not knowing that there are many others just like you.

Our second message is that you are very brave. You are brave to pick up this book and read this far. More than anything—because you think these thoughts might mean something important and could be dangerous—you work to keep these thoughts out of your mind. And we are sure that you have tried everything to do just that. So buying this book and reading about the subject is an act of courage.

Struggling the way you have, you have probably discovered a very frustrating and important truth. Trying to keep thoughts out of your mind doesn't work for you. *It doesn't work for anybody.*

And so we start with another basic truth: If you continue to do what you've always done, you are going to get what you've always got (Forsythe and Eifert 2007). In other words, if you want a different outcome, you will have to try a different method. We would like you to start with the realization that *there is nothing wrong with you, but there is something quite wrong with your method.* And here is where this book can be helpful. We believe that giving your thoughts a name, helping you understand that you are not alone, and addressing the thoughts without shame and fear will go a long way toward reducing your misery. But that is certainly not all. You are going to learn what we now know about unwanted intrusive thoughts, the various types of them, what keeps them going, and the very best approaches to living a life without the misery of these stuck thoughts.

Helpful Fact: There is nothing wrong with you, just the way you are dealing with your thoughts.

This is typical of the notes we receive from people who have read accurate information about unwanted intrusive thoughts.

I've had an anxiety disorder for more than eleven years, and I've had intrusive thoughts much of those times. My therapists haven't had much understanding of them, and as I'm sure you're very aware, it can be crippling to try to tell someone about them.

Reading your article on intrusive thoughts, and especially how you clearly stated that they are often violent or sexual, has given me so much more hope. I thought this was my sick, twisted mind—that no one would accept. Seeing it given a name, and written so clearly, is revelatory, and has given me the confidence to seek more help.

Good help for unwanted intrusive thoughts is hard to find and access. Talking with sympathetic friends or family who do not understand is usually not helpful and can often make things worse. There is no other modern self-help book devoted exclusively to this issue. Even if you are able to overcome fears about disclosing your thoughts, you may not be receiving well-informed help. And, unfortunately, this problem rarely goes away on its own.

You may have talked to a therapist about your unwanted intrusive thoughts. Or you may even have a diagnosed condition of which unwanted intrusive thoughts are a component. If you aren't getting relief from your unwanted intrusive thoughts, this book is for you. Not all therapists know the most effective ways to deal with unwanted intrusive thoughts, or you may be hesitant to talk about them. This book provides a unique, practical, working program to lead you to a life that is free from the dread, demoralization, and suffering that these thoughts now bring.

How to Get the Most out of This Book

Remember that knowledge is power, and the more you know about unwanted intrusive thoughts, the better you will be able to free yourself from the misery they bring. This book is meant to be read from beginning to end, and we are firmly convinced that you will get the most benefit from it if you do that. We understand that you are anxious to start the process of ridding yourself of unwanted intrusive thoughts. You will start learning how in the very first pages, continuing through each subsequent chapter. So we would like you to consider the initial chapters of this book as the initial steps of your recovery. In fact, you might find that the first few chapters are all you need to get over them.

Chapter 1 is filled with facts, including the latest information about unwanted intrusive thoughts. Chapter 2 provides a comprehensive description of the various types of unwanted intrusive thoughts. Chapter 3 debunks the myths that contribute to unwanted intrusive thoughts, and in chapter 4, we share the answers to questions that people often ask. In chapter 5, you will learn about how your brain makes these intrusions such a bother. We also show how certain passing thoughts become stuck and then turn into unwanted intrusive thoughts. We explain why your best attempts to cope have been unsuccessful and why many of the traditional anxiety management techniques can actually be counterproductive in chapter 6. Good explanations are good treatment.

> **Helpful Fact:** Just knowing accurate information about unwanted intrusive thoughts will make them feel less distressing.

In chapters 7 through 9, you will see specific suggestions for the changes in beliefs and attitude required and the way to train your mind, brain, and body to react in an entirely different manner. Most chapters build on the knowledge base and practical information presented previously. Knowing what you know and applying it systematically will get you over the pain, bewilderment, frustration, and terror that these intrusive thoughts can bring. Chapter 10 is a straightforward discussion of when self-help is not likely to be enough and it is time to seek professional help. Finally, in keeping with our belief that many of us take ourselves and our thoughts too seriously, we have added a light-hearted appendix with a recipe of essentially what not to do about intrusive thoughts.

Will recovery be easy? Probably not, because you will have to unlearn many unhelpful thinking habits, as well as your automatic emotional reactions to these thoughts and the ways you try to avoid them. You will be learning new, more helpful ways of responding to these false tyrants in your mind. You will need to practice these new ways of addressing your thoughts, as they do not feel natural at first. But we will also explain how to practice, and the ways to retrain your emotional reactions. And, just as you can't learn to dance by only reading about dance steps, we will encourage you to get onto the "dance floor" of your mind and work out your missteps as they occur.

Will recovery be difficult? Probably, yes. But consider the alternative and the quality of the life you are living right now. It will not be as difficult as you may think if you truly understand that your current beliefs about these thoughts and what they mean are not supported by what we now know about them. It is not what you think: you are in no danger from weird, scary, and disturbing unwanted thoughts. *The answer is learning an entirely new relationship to thoughts, which is being neither scared nor ashamed of them.* Gradually, you will learn to tame those bullies in your head and live a life that is free from their torment.

CHAPTER 1

Recovering from Unwanted Intrusive Thoughts

Recovering from unwanted intrusive thoughts is multifaceted. It begins with knowing what thoughts mean and what they don't. It involves an understanding of how particular thoughts become stuck and keep repeating. It encompasses an explanation of why your harmless intrusive thoughts feel so disturbing and dangerous. And it means learning to substitute your present (unhelpful) ways of coping with an approach that will train your brain, body, and emotions to react differently. Your goal, of course, is to eliminate the fear, frustrations, guilt, and misery that unwanted intrusive thoughts can bring. Each of these facets constitutes a step on the way to recovery. Each step provides some relief, and all the steps together constitute the journey to recovery upon which we now embark.

Just about everyone has intrusive thoughts. They are uninvited thoughts that jump into the mind and do not seem to be part of the ongoing flow of intentional thinking. Intrusive thoughts are common, but for most people they are quickly forgotten and create minimal or no discomfort. For someone who isn't struggling with or worrying about intrusive thoughts, they provide weird, uncomfortable, or even funny moments ... and then they are over. Sometimes they startle. Most intrusive thoughts—no matter how bizarre or repugnant—occupy only a few moments. People rarely mention them or think about them again. They are just not worth mentioning (unless they are really funny).

Helpful Fact: Almost everyone has passing intrusive thoughts.

Here is an intrusive thought that I had while writing this paragraph: *I hope we lose power in this storm so I don't have to keep working.* The thought went winging by, and I made nothing of it. But here is the thing: if I *were* worried about my mind or my motives or my thoughts, I might be embarrassed to write this. I might worry about what the thought could mean about me. Shouldn't I be enjoying my work? Does this mean I should retire? Am I getting burned-out? Could I be depressed if I want an excuse not to write this book? Why am I not concentrating? Do I *really* want to lose power? What is wrong with me that I thought that? Or, I might wonder that perhaps I have received a special message, and my thought means that I really am going to lose power, in which case, I should probably go get candles right now. Instead, I do nothing at all. The moment passes. It was just a thought not worth even considering what it means. I go back to writing.

There are times when anyone can be reminded of a previous intrusive thought and shake his or her head, *Oh I remember that this is the elevator where I had that utterly weird experience of thinking that I was going to suddenly shout out an obscenity.* Sometimes—for a while—elevators and thoughts about shouting out obscenities get temporarily stuck to each other. One is associated with the other. It means nothing. The human mind just makes associations like that automatically. The experience, while strange, is unimportant and goes away.

An unwanted intrusive thought starts as just an ordinary intrusive thought, weird, funny, or repugnant as it may be. But not wanting the thought, worrying about it, or fighting with it stops it from passing quickly. Chances are, you don't want it because you are upset or turned off by the content. But that is just the beginning. Because you worry about it, reject it, and try to push it out of your mind, it pushes back and becomes a recurring thought or image. After a while, it starts to redirect your attention: It starts arriving with a "whoosh," and feels awful, disgusting, or dreaded. It contains an urgent feeling of needing to get rid of it. The content of many unwanted intrusive thoughts is aggressive, sexual, taboo, anxiety-provoking, or self-derogatory. An unwanted intrusive thought sometimes feels like an impulse to perform an unwanted action. Other times, it feels impossibly stuck in your head. Your efforts to deal with it become all-encompassing and take up so much time, mental energy, and focus that your quality of life is degraded. Unwanted intrusive thoughts tend to recur repeatedly and seem to increase in intensity over time. Eventually, along with an increase in the frequency and intensity of the thoughts themselves, you might start to doubt and fear your own safety, intentions, morality, self-control, and sanity.

Natural Voices of the Mind

Our mind has many natural voices, and their interplay makes our mental lives interesting and colorful. We can all identify an internal critical voice that stands guard, issuing judgments and comments, most of which we would never say out loud. We also have voices that monitor feedback from others, check on our physical well-being, calculate how much time we have left to finish a task, and let us know what we are feeling when we tune in. There are many more. The voices are natural parts of our mind as we divide up the tasks of the day, make choices, and adapt to the demands of daily living.

In the case of unwanted intrusive thoughts, there are three voices that are particularly relevant. Their messages and interactions work to maintain the problem. By providing distinct examples of these voices, we hope to make it easier for you to observe these same processes in your own mind. And this will help you make the fundamental shift in your relationship with your thoughts that relieves the distress.

So we introduce you to the voices that we call "Worried Voice," "False Comfort," and "Wise Mind." As you proceed through this book, we will present a variety of dialogues and commentaries involving these voices. Each of these voices sends messages that are consistent with its name. We will help you understand how best to relate to them when they pop up and intrude into your mind.

Let's start with Worried Voice, the voice of frightening imaginings. Worried Voice is the voice of "What if?" Worried

Voice articulates the fears and doubts and misguided conclusions that predict tragedies and awful outcomes. This voice can seem irrational, ridiculous, even perverse, or downright crazy. Sometimes Worried Voice issues strange or urgent warnings. It interrupts, annoys, scares, and talks back. Worried Voice raises anxiety. Worried Voice is often the first voice to react to an intrusive thought or new sensation.

Next is False Comfort. False Comfort invariably follows the "What if?" of Worried Voice. False Comfort is disturbed by these questions and tries to remove the discomfort. We call this voice False Comfort because it never achieves its goal. It often gives brief relief and the illusion of rationality. But it does not ultimately silence Worried Voice. In fact, it does the opposite. False Comfort almost always triggers yet another what-if or doubt from Worried Voice. False Comfort is actually so disturbed and frightened by Worried Voice that it continuously tries to argue, control, avoid, suppress, reassure, reason with, neutralize, or work around whatever Worried Voice comes up with.

False Comfort tries hard but ultimately fails to lower anxiety. It often gets angry at or ashamed of Worried Voice and wishes it would just go away. It is afraid that some of the thoughts that pop up in Worried Voice indicate craziness, danger, annoyance, perversion, being out of control, or being disgusting. When unwanted intrusive thoughts happen, Worried Voice and False Comfort invariably launch into a back-and-forth argument. *This is the commentary that is part and parcel of every unwanted intrusive thought.*

Helpful Fact: Your commentary, in the form of the back-and-forth arguments between Worried Voice and False Comfort, can be the most distressing aspect of your unwanted intrusive thought.

Finally, we welcome Wise Mind, who watches the constant arguments between Worried Voice and False Comfort from afar, saying relatively little. Wise Mind is calm, unimpressed, and unaffected. It knows Worried Voice can't help itself and that False Comfort truly thinks it is helping. However, Wise Mind knows that False Comfort is actually spurring Worried Voice on, keeping the process going without realizing it. In contrast, Wise Mind is disentangled, free of effort, and accepting of uncertainty. It is curious and sometimes even amused by things that upset the others.

Wise Mind demonstrates mindful compassionate awareness. Mindfulness is a state of open and active attention to the present, moment by moment. It involves the experience of observing your thoughts, feelings, and sensations without judgment or evaluation. A mindful attitude is made possible because there is a part of you that can stand back and look at your experiences—in real time—with perspective. We will show you that a mindful attitude is enormously helpful in ridding yourself of unwanted intrusive thoughts, and we will explain how to apply this attitude when needed. Here is an example of how the three voices react to a thought:

Worried Voice: That kitten is so cute and vulnerable. What if I strangled it? It would be so easy.

False Comfort: You would never do that!

Worried Voice: Look—my fingers just fit around its neck.

False Comfort: Don't be ridiculous. You are kind and loving!

Worried Voice: How do you know that? I had that surge of road rage yesterday. What if I can't help myself?

False Comfort: You just felt angry; you didn't do anything. Just stop thinking that. It won't happen.

Worried Voice: There is always a first time, and I wonder if there is something sick inside of me. Why else would I have such a thought?

False Comfort: Just think about something else. Let's get away from the kitten. This is crazy! You are thinking crazy thoughts.

Worried Voice: So you think I have crazy thoughts?

Wise Mind: Let me step in here, please. These are just thoughts. I watch the two of you fight. I'm observing your commentary. I notice the more you argue, the more upset you get. And the more it seems like a real issue that needs attention. It is actually a wild intrusion of a thought that can happen to anyone and essentially means nothing. What would happen if you just let them be? Let them remain as thoughts.

Helpful Fact: Observing and letting go of your commentary will go a long way toward gaining some relief from your intrusive thoughts.

Why Thoughts Get Stuck

A psychologist named Daniel Wegner (1994) studied the phenomenon that he called the "ironic process of the mind." Another psychologist Lee Baer (2001) called the same process the "imp of the mind," referring to a short story by Edgar Allen Poe entitled "The Imp of the Perverse." The phenomenon is that when you try not to think of something, you end up thinking about it even more. It's ironic: your mind can be quite impish! Here is a simple way to experience this process:

EXERCISE: Observing Your Own Ironic Process

This demonstration will take less than ten minutes, and it consists of two parts.

Part 1

Set a timer for two minutes. Sit comfortably, close your eyes, and pay attention to what you think, feel, hear, and smell. You may think about anything you want—anything at all—except for one thing. Under no circumstances should you think about *carrots.* Not the word *carrot,* not the smell of carrots, not the taste. Nothing with carrots in it—no carrot cake, no carrot salad, and certainly no Bugs Bunny! It might help to stay away from the color orange as well. Now start the timer, and do your best to keep your thoughts away from carrots.

After the timer goes off, ask yourself how well you did. Now, most people will report that they failed to be completely free of carrots. The effort to *not* think about carrots backfires. In fact, the effort itself is doomed to failure. The more you try to rid your mind of carrots, the more insistent the thought becomes. So trying not to think about carrots is a form of thinking about them.

Part 2

In this portion of the exercise, you will set your timer for five minutes. Your task is to try to keep your mind completely free of carrots for five minutes. As in the first part of the exercise, sit comfortably and give yourself permission to think about anything at all except carrots. Start the timer, and each time you think of carrots, you must reset the timer back to five minutes. Your task is simply to go five minutes without thinking of carrots. Be honest! Ready, get set, go!

Now look at what happened. Most people report that they think of carrots after just a few seconds, so they reset the timer. But then it happens again, and the timer is once again reset. After a while, the task starts to seem impossible. You become frustrated, annoyed, and even angry. And each time the thought comes back sooner and sooner. Almost no one is able to go five minutes, and so you end the exercise with the timer still ticking away.

But let's look at what you have done. *You have created a "stuck" thought!* The content of the thought is *carrots,* which is about as uncontroversial and non-upsetting as can be, but that thought has become stuck in your mind. You really couldn't care less about carrots one way or the other. It is your attempt to follow the assignment that has now created all those thoughts about carrots. Your attempt to control your mind has backfired. The simple truth is that what you resist tends to persist. This is the basic paradox—the ironic process—at work in making unwanted intrusive thoughts so persistent. *Thoughts stick because of the energy you expend to fight them.* Your assignment was to fight the thoughts, but they fight back! *Worried Voice:* Carrots make me think about sex. Anything shaped like that does. What kind of person thinks like that? I'm disgusting.

False Comfort: This is supposed to be a neutral topic. Think about something neutral.

Worried Voice: I can't help it.

False Comfort: Just distract yourself. Put your mind on another topic.

Worried Voice: I have these thoughts all the time, you know. Maybe I truly am a disgusting person.

False Comfort: Why am I stuck with you? Why won't you just shut up and listen to me?

False Comfort would like Worried Voice to just stop offering unwanted intrusive thoughts. It tries to help Worried Voice stop, but it doesn't work. False Comfort objects to every one of those thoughts. But Worried Voice just can't help where its mind goes.

> **Helpful Fact:** Thoughts stick because of the energy you expend to fight them.

Thoughts That Get Stuck

The thoughts you most do not want to have are the ones that get stuck. Of course! That makes so much sense. So we find that people who are struggling with violent thoughts are people who value gentleness, find violence abhorrent, and live nonviolent caring lives. People who have felt assaulted by thoughts of hurting others are loving people. That is why these thoughts are fought—and then become stuck. Similarly, people who believe that all vulnerable people and living things should be protected are people who fight common intrusive thoughts that sometimes involve actions like abusing children, throwing cats out windows, and dropping babies. These are the thoughts you fight—and because you fight them, they stick. If you are someone with strong religious beliefs, you sometimes come up with blasphemous thoughts and worry thoughts about not being faithful. These are the thoughts you fight ... and they stick.

Thoughts about chairs and fruit salad and trees don't stick because they are neutral thoughts. Neutral thoughts are not fought because no one cares about them—so they don't stick.

So the content of unwanted intrusive thoughts is the *opposite* of what you want to be thinking about. It is the opposite of your values, the opposite of your wishes, and the opposite of your character. It is the opposite of you.

Helpful Fact: Unwanted intrusive thoughts get stuck because you inadvertently fuel them by trying to push them away.

Intrusive Thoughts Versus Impulses

You might be afraid that you are going to act on your intrusive thoughts and actually do the things that run through your mind. Because unwanted intrusive thoughts tend to get stuck and repeat when you struggle with them, they increase in intensity. Every time you fight them, they fight back, so there is a very intense feeling that goes with them—a whoosh of fear—and sometimes shame, disgust, or anger. This can make them feel like impulses—as if somehow you were being pushed, impelled, or provoked to do something out of control, ridiculous, or dangerous. This feeling can be very disturbing, but you need not worry: it is an illusion, a paper tiger, a false alarm. Your brain is issuing warnings where none are needed.

Suffering about unwanted intrusive thoughts is a disorder of *overcontrol,* not undercontrol. (Undercontrol disorders are sometimes known as impulsivity.) Disorders of overcontrol are usually accompanied by a problem with doubt or uncertainty. Put the two together—trying to control those things that you cannot control (in this case, your thoughts) and wanting to be absolutely, 100 percent sure that nothing bad will happen—and you have the formula for unwanted intrusive thoughts.

People who are impulsive act first and think later. People with unwanted intrusive thoughts are over-thinkers. The problem is that unwanted intrusive thoughts may well be experienced as if they were impulses, and you might even feel that you have to work hard to control yourself. We will address this issue later on, when we discuss anxious thinking and the altered state of consciousness it brings about. For now, however, you can rest assured that impulses and intrusive thoughts are opposite sides of a continuum: they just can't be any more different, despite how they might feel.

Helpful Fact: Despite how they might feel, impulses and intrusive thoughts couldn't be more different.

When Intrusive Thoughts Are Likely to Happen

Unwanted intrusive thoughts fluctuate in frequency and intensity. As you understand that intrusive thoughts are thoughts that are stuck in your mind, then you realize that this is most likely to occur when your mind is especially "sticky." There are a host of factors—some psychological and others physiological—that affect thought "stickiness."

You might have already discovered some of the factors. People are much more prone to unwanted intrusive thoughts when they are fatigued, have slept poorly, or are in a bad mood (anxious, crabby, irritable, feeling down or blue). If you are a woman who is menstruating, hormonal changes during your cycle can increase the frequency and intensity of your unwanted intrusive thoughts. Certain drugs, such as caffeine, over-the-counter drugs, and physician-prescribed medications, such as steroids and asthma medications, can as well. The day after consuming alcohol is usually a sticky day for most people. And some kinds of marijuana produce instant stickiness. Stickiness can fluctuate during the day, and often is the worst in the morning (almost as soon as you are awake) and when you are lying down to sleep.

Worried Voice: Oh, no! I drank too much last night and feel hungover. This is not a good day to go shopping. What if I have those awful thoughts about the people in the store? I have a headache, so I think I will stay home and avoid being around people.

False Comfort: That's okay. Why add stress when you feel bad? We can go tomorrow.

Worried Voice: I just know I am going to get stuck in a line and start having those terrible thoughts about the person in front of me. It always happens on days like this. I will wait till tomorrow.

Wise Mind: You know that some days our mind is stickier than other days, and it is easy to get worried about having sticky thoughts on those days. But avoiding makes the mind even stickier. It suggests that you are fragile or impaired on "sticky mind" days. You feel resentful, and you miss out on things. And you give yourself a message that somehow sticky thoughts are more dangerous on those days. Go on out. Shopping thoughts are just thoughts even in sticky times.

Any situation that is uncertain and has "high stakes" is a perfect place for stickiness of the mind to increase. As soon as it seems important to know something 100 percent for sure, that is where the unwanted intrusive thoughts will find their opening.

For example, if, while cleaning, you have an intrusive thought that you may pour cleaning fluid into the flower pot, the worst that can happen is a dead plant. Take that same intrusive thought and imagine that you might feed the cleaning fluid to your baby. Now the stakes are instantly higher, and the chance for the thought to get stuck increases. For the same reason, the mind can be stickier on an airplane than at home.

In this example, Worried Voice has an intrusive thought about something that is very unlikely to happen, but whose stakes are very high. That scares False Comfort. They begin to argue. Wise Mind adds a few thoughts.

Worried Voice: Maybe I should wash my hands after shaking that guy's hand. I don't know him. Oh God, he looks like he's an international traveler. Maybe he picked up dengue fever, or maybe even Ebola!

False Comfort: I hadn't even thought of it. But it's always a safe thing to wash your hands. I don't think he has Ebola—I thought it was eliminated. The outbreak is over. And he looks okay. And I don't think dengue can get here unless a mosquito goes on the plane. What would be the chances of that?

Worried Voice: You never know. I realize now I have a sore on my hand. What if the virus got into me?

False Comfort: That is so unlikely! There is almost no chance of that happening.

Worried Voice: And if it does?

False Comfort: You are making me nervous. Just stop it! Try to think of something else. Or wash once and be done with it!

Worried Voice: But we don't want to get sick, and Ebola is a killer! Why risk that?

Wise Mind: Look, you guys, nothing in life is risk-free—really, nothing. You can live with it or drive yourselves nuts around it. It's up to you.

Wise Mind is providing the voice of acceptance and surrender to these thoughts. It points out that seeking a perfect, 100 percent risk-free world is useless and self-defeating and that both Worried Voice and False Comfort could lead happier lives if they stopped fighting and allowed their thoughts to exist without debate.

Trigger: Personal Experiences

Of course, if you personally experience a really awful event, that high-impact event can trigger the emergence of unwanted intrusive thoughts. Here is an example:

We were horrified this past March with the shocking suicide of my younger sister. She seemed to be the most upbeat person you could ever imagine, with everything going for her, and seemed perfectly "normal" to us. I think this is where my intrusive thoughts, *Oh God if she did this, maybe I will too,* came from. I found myself doing everything I could to make sure that would not happen. This had been counterproductive for my anxiety. I found myself looking at YouTube videos about suicide to make sure I would never do anything like that. That was a great mistake.

Here is how Worried and False Comfort might react to a personal tragedy. Notice how their dialogue just continues to increase distress.

Worried Voice: Dad just died of a heart attack. He was only sixty-three. That could be us. Look how out of breath we are. That could be a sign.

False Comfort: We just went to the cardiologist. She said everything is fine.

Worried Voice: But things can happen suddenly. Look at that runner who died while he was in a race.

False Comfort: We can't be going to the doctor all the time. She already thinks we are hypochondriacs. Let's just take our pulse and blood pressure at home every day. We feel better when it is okay.

Worried Voice: How can we be sure the machine is working right? I think maybe several times a day.

False Comfort: Don't be silly! Of course it is working. Okay, let's do it twice a day.

Worried Voice: Don't just humor me. This is important, we could die.

False Comfort: You just need to trust things will be okay.

Worried Voice: There must be a reason I keep thinking about death. I can't *just trust* anyone. What if I have a *sixth sense?*

Highly upsetting, shocking, or dramatic events can raise the level of anxiety and even seem to change the probabilities of unrelated bad things happening. Events like these can make terrible occurrences seem more likely, and so you work even harder to make sure they never happen to you.

Traumatic events can be major triggers of unwanted intrusive thoughts, and we will speak about this in chapter 2 when we discuss the types of unwanted intrusive thoughts.

Trigger: The Media and Current Events

It is commonplace for people to have outbreaks of intrusive thoughts after the media report a human-caused disaster. Whenever there is a report of an event that is awful, we all gain an increased sense that horrible events really do occur, and it is not uncommon to wonder if perhaps we could do something similar. These wonderings may even include imagining it happening.

If you are already disturbed by your thoughts and working hard to keep them out of your mind, reading about a mother who murders her children or a gunman who shoots innocent children can very well trigger an intense spike of anxiety. This is because you are *sensitized to that thought,* not because you are going to do that. Sensitization can be compared to an allergy. An allergic person has a strong reaction to substances that cause little response in others. In the same way, you react with great intensity to certain thoughts that others don't. And, just as you try to avoid things you are allergic to, sensitized thoughts push you to work hard to avoid, crowd out, and try to banish your own intrusive thoughts. Since thoughts stick and start to feel like impulses in *direct proportion to the effort you use to keep them from your mind,* then, of course, media reports can intensify your own unwanted thoughts. Sensitization has a normal biological basis, which we will explain later.

If your stuck thought concerns the possibility of doing something impulsive and dangerous while driving, then reading about a mother who caused a fatal accident by driving the wrong way on a highway will start the process that makes your own thoughts feel all the more dangerous. Remember that your fearful reaction to reading about an incident initiates the process of trying to fight the thought, and the ironic process of the mind can take over and increase your disturbing thoughts dramatically.

So, if a suicidal pilot takes down a plane full of passengers and your intrusive thoughts have concerned a sudden impulsive suicide that seems contrary to your own wishes, you might redouble your efforts to stop the unwanted intrusions. You might even start to hide ropes and knives, even though you are not actually suicidal.

If you are plagued by thoughts of bad things that could happen and your need to prepare for them or watch for them—however unlikely—then reports of rare but scary events, like plane crashes or shark attacks, can trigger more unwanted thoughts and more attempts to control those thoughts. Fears of fatal or serious diseases, like Ebola or AIDS, work in a similar way. You are trying to keep those thoughts out of your mind, and when the news reports are filled with descriptions of the disease—and especially the way it can be transmitted despite rigorous infection control attempts—anxious distress increases. Then you try to fight the thoughts with even more effort, and your what-if, stuck thoughts begin to feel more and more like real possibilities.

And of, course, we are most afraid of things that would be terrible if they did happen, regardless of how unlikely or even virtually impossible they may be. This is another time when anxious people confuse the difference between stakes and odds. So if the stakes are high (like death, humiliation, or jail), then it really doesn't seem to matter how unlikely it might be. And, of course, the media tend to focus on those events that are awful, dramatic, and traumatic.

There are people who report that they started having unwanted intrusive thoughts while watching a movie such as *The Exorcist* or *The Matrix.* Here is what usually happens: You are watching the movie, and, suddenly, out of the blue, you get a terrifying thought related to the movie that scares the heck out of you. The thought keeps coming back and triggering more fear, so you become involved in an ongoing and repeated battle with your thoughts. And, as we have already said, fighting with your thoughts that way is the same as handing them a victory.

But the fight seems natural and necessary, and so you keep it up. After all, you don't know any other way to act, and you feel an automatic sense of fear and dread and frustration.

Here are Worried Voice and False Comfort at it again. Wise Mind is not around.

Worried Voice: Maybe I am possessed? What if that is the reason I keep coming up with these terrible thoughts?

False Comfort: Don't be silly. Possession is just in the movies.

Worried Voice: No, some churches really do believe souls can be possessed. Who is to say they are not right?

False Comfort: This is just an idea the movie put in your head. Stop thinking about it! You know how it upsets me.

Worried Voice: Yeah, well, you never know. It could be. You can't prove it.

With movies like *The Matrix*, people sometimes get stuck on the thoughts that maybe reality isn't at all what it seems and that it's impossible to know the nature of reality for other people. It can seem like suddenly everything about reality is not certain at all, and you may even have the thought that you are losing touch with reality. It triggers fears that keep on returning. With movies like *The Exorcist,* the thought might be about the possibility of being possessed by evil and wondering if that could happen, if it could already be happening, and if you could possibly harm the people you love. Since these ideas feel so frightening to you, you fight them as well. And—as you probably have already guessed—this ensures that they become stuck in your mind.

The answer here is not to avoid the possibility of this happening by avoiding media—although that is often the first instinct of people struggling with unwanted intrusive thoughts. We will show you how to enjoy movies, TV, and the Internet, whether or not they temporarily stimulate intrusive thoughts.

Helpful Fact: Contrary to common sense, reducing your effort to avoid intrusive thoughts will often lead to less distress.

In this chapter, we have reviewed some important facts about unwanted intrusive thoughts that may have calmed some of your fears and already started you on the road to recovery. Intrusive thoughts, however weird or scary, are universal and unimportant. Unwanted intrusive thoughts get stuck because you inadvertently fuel them by trying to banish them. They fluctuate in intensity and frequency based on the fuel they receive—triggering events in the real world or the *stickiness* of your mind due to fatigue, mood, or anxiety—and, ironically, by the amount of effort you expend to try to counteract, avoid, or suppress them. Most importantly, they are not impulses, and you are not out of control.

In the next chapter, we will describe the different types of unwanted intrusive thoughts.

CHAPTER 2

Varieties of Intrusive Thoughts

You are now going to read about the many different types of unwanted intrusive thoughts. This chapter includes some very specific and explicit examples. You may find that reading it might trigger increased anxiety and distress because you have put so much effort and energy into trying *not* to think these thoughts. But we know that whatever temporary upset you might feel, finding your own particular variety of unwanted intrusive thoughts will be extremely helpful.

We give specific examples for several reasons. You may be so ashamed or afraid of your unwanted intrusive thoughts that you have never expressed them to anyone. Or, you may have spoken about them indirectly, leaving out the details or putting them in more acceptable terms. There is nothing shocking to us about these thoughts—we know they are harmless. But unless we go into details, you run the risk of believing that your own particular thoughts are different, more serious, or more odious, or even worse, that what we are saying does not apply to you. So we invite you to find yourself in these pages and know that you are not alone. If reading these examples makes you uncomfortable, remember that the goal is to find a path away from your suffering, and there are times that you will need to accept some additional discomfort in order to make that journey. Finding yourself in these descriptions will be a huge relief because we are talking about good, sane people—people who are suffering from these thoughts, who are not crazy, perverted, or dangerous.

Second, there are some people who don't realize that they are having intrusive thoughts. They only know that they feel terrible about ideas, impulses, or certain aspects of their character, just like one of our clients who said, "Whatever it is, it must be the product of a majorly twisted mind." We would like you to recognize your own particular issue in this chapter and to say, "Bingo! That is me! That is what happens! That is my problem! Now I know I'm not alone, and I can do something about it."

These examples were provided by people who are just like you. Good people, gentle people, kind people—but people who have stuck thoughts that cause them pain. As you read this chapter, pay attention to your own feelings. You might feel scared, disgusted, repelled, skeptical, or even perversely fascinated. Or you may feel relieved as you put your own thoughts in perspective. Any of these reactions and feelings are to be expected and are okay. Take your time. Go at your own pace.

If you are worried that you can catch someone else's intrusive thought, it may help to know that people tend to stay in their own categories, although they may wander a bit from one specific content of intrusive thought to another. We have heard people say they would happily trade their kind of unwanted intrusive thoughts for some other kind that seems on the surface less awful.

But they are all awful to the person who is having them, and they are all functioning essentially the same way in the mind. One is no more reprehensible, meaningful, or important than another. Remember that there is no danger in reading this chapter, only discomfort and possibly a lot of relief.

Morally Repugnant Thoughts

The first types of unwanted intrusive thoughts are about things that are morally repugnant. They include harming and self-harming, sexual, impure religious, and disgust-causing thoughts.

Harming and Self-Harming Thoughts

The most common morally repugnant thoughts are of harming, either yourself or someone else. Part of the misery of having these thoughts is that your thoughts often center on harming innocent, helpless, or beloved individuals. And the self-harming thoughts are both frightening and bewildering because there is no conscious, intentional wish to hurt yourself or others.

Here are some examples of harming and self-harming unwanted intrusive thoughts.

My daughter saw a scary movie about the Columbine killings, and now she keeps having intrusive thoughts about killing her friends or family members with knives. She wants all the knives in the house hidden because they scare her so much. She is the kindest, most gentle person you could ever know, who loves and cares about every person she meets. The thoughts are obviously causing her a great deal of anxiety because she is afraid she is going to act on them.

After Sandy Hook, I started thinking that I wish my child were there. But I love my son, and why would that thought even occur to me?

I can't go out on balconies because every time I do, I have the thought, What is stopping me from jumping off? I could do it right now. I get completely panicked, especially if the railing is low and I could actually climb over it. Do you think I am secretly suicidal? I don't even feel depressed.

Every time I see a rope or even something that I think might be a rope, I have a sudden image of myself hanging from a hook in my bedroom. Why is this happening? I can't make it stop.

After I had the baby, I was afraid to pick her up because I kept thinking I might drop her—or even God forbid—throw her out the window or down the stairs.

Forbidden Sexual Thoughts

Forbidden sexual thoughts are also common and can include thinking about sexual relations with relatives and children as well as unsavory or extramarital relations.

I've been having horrible obsessive thoughts that I can't let go. They are always hanging over my head, even at work. It's making my anxiety terrible—I wake up with a pounding in my chest because I know I'm going to be having these obsessive thoughts all day, and they're just so awful. I can't even watch TV because I feel like a pedophile, but I would never do anything to a child or anyone for that matter. I'm really scared. What if I am a pedophile?

For some bizarre reason, I had the thought, What if I were attracted to my brother? Now I can barely look at him and won't go to the beach with him because I am afraid to see him in a bathing suit. He knows I am avoiding him, but of course I can't tell him why.

I am happily married, but I keep thinking about having sex with this man I spoke to once while I was waiting for the bus. He isn't even attractive. Does this mean I don't love my husband?

Impure or Blasphemous Religious Thoughts

These can be particularly painful because the people who have these thoughts are sincerely spiritual, religious, good-natured individuals. It is initially difficult to see that trying to banish these thoughts is actually a distortion of religion, not the practice of religion.

When I am saying my prayers, I get the feeling that I am not in the right frame of mind and that God can tell I am not really believing what I am saying. So even while I am praying, I find myself thinking about sinning, and the sins I am thinking about are getting worse and worse. I pray harder to get my mind off the topics, but then I hear blasphemous things in my mind. I think I am being punished for a past transgression, but I do not know what it was, and I cannot pray for proper forgiveness. So I am praying more and more. I fear my soul is lost. I tried to talk to my minister, but he did not seem to understand.

As I was entering church a few months ago, I suddenly thought, You don't really believe in God; who are you kidding? Now I am doubting everything I ever believed—even what is right and wrong. My priest says even the saints had doubts, but I can't stand this.

When I am in a holy place like a sanctuary, especially if it is quiet, I start feeling as if I am about to shout out hateful things.

Disgust-Causing Intrusions

These are thoughts that bother and disgust you, and take away from pleasure in life or the anticipation of pleasure. They usually occur when you engage in something pleasurable. These can include the belief that you will think about sex with your parent when making love to your girlfriend. As a result, you avoid doing the pleasurable act.

I know I'm a lesbian. I want to have a girlfriend and be part of a relationship. But every time I imagine kissing a girl and getting sexually intimate, I get the thought in my mind about having sex with my sister. It's a terrible thought, and it keeps me from having the relationship that I want.

I suddenly get the thought that I'm going to imagine having oral sex with my mother when I'm hooking up with a girl. I have to somehow neutralize that thought or else I'm afraid it will ruin my performance. I get so worried about it when I'm with a girl that I get drunk and almost blackout. Most of the time the girl drops me, and the few times I've actually hooked up, I couldn't remember any of the details.

Whenever I am in a restaurant, I have the sudden image of someone spitting into my plate just before they bring it to me. I know it is ridiculous; I think I saw this scene in a movie years ago, but then when the food arrives, I can't eat.

One time my girlfriend said she hoped my penis couldn't break off. I know she was joking, but I am so upset at her for saying that, I can't get it out of my mind. It has ruined everything.

My dog licks her private parts and then licks my daughter. I can't stand it, and I can't stop thinking about all the germs and secretions that are getting on my daughter.

"Big Issue" Thoughts

The next type of intrusive thought falls in the category of *big issues* and involves continual episodes of trying to answer questions about these issues that are essentially unanswerable. The most common ones involve the questions of uncertainty and lack of guarantees in life, the nature of reality, the purpose of life, and how can you know if you really, really believe or feel something. These questions seem really important and almost always involve questions with many dimensions and no definite answers.

Uncertainty and Unknowability Thoughts

Being unwilling to accept that we cannot know or guarantee the future leads to this kind of preoccupation.

I have to know my kids will be safe. How can anyone live without this? I can't stand even the thought that something could happen to them.

Questioning Reality

It is one thing to have a truly philosophical curiosity about the nature of reality and quite another to be extremely upset and constantly preoccupied by such questions that do not have clear answers.

What is the nature of reality? How can I know if your reality is the same as mine?

I can't get it out of my head that this actually could be a shared illusion, everything we think is reality could be a mental projection, and there is no way to tell. I am stuck on this, and I keep trying to find a way to prove it.

Purpose-of-Life Thoughts

Some people have intense and persistent trouble knowing we will die and the implications of that. As a result, they feel compelled to repeatedly address this question every time a thought about it pops up.

What is the purpose of life? Is there an afterlife; what if there isn't?

I don't understand how people live knowing they will die and not knowing what happens after that. I want to believe in heaven, but I really can't make myself believe it. So if this is all there is, we should spend every minute in a meaningful way, but I can't figure out the point of all of it. I have been reading philosophy and religious writings and talking with people who seem to have found peaceful ways of living with this, but I can't stop thinking about this and feeling lost. I am thinking a psychotherapist could have insights into the purpose of life. "This is all meaningless" keeps popping into my mind. Maybe it is true.

Questioning Beliefs

Our minds are filled with inconsistencies, ambivalences, and constant change. Some people find this very disturbing and continually search for certainty.

What do I really believe or feel about this?

I have this friend whom I spend a lot of time with, and I really love her. But sometimes she really annoys me, or I don't feel like calling her back. But then when I see her, I am always upset with myself for having been angry at her because she really is a wonderful person. Maybe I am really jealous of her—or maybe I really am threatened by her because I am not as nice as she is—because I keep having these thoughts when I am not actually with her. Do you think I am deceiving myself? Maybe I should not spend as much time with her? Or should I tell her when she annoys me? But that would upset her...

Nonsensical Thoughts

The third type of intrusive thoughts are ones that seem nonsensical, require rigorous mental checks when there doesn't seem to any reason to do so, or involve incessant doubting.

Losing-Your-Mind Thoughts

Some intrusive thoughts just seem utterly ridiculous as they whoosh into the mind for no apparent reason. They often feel like products of a mind on the edge of sanity. They are not.

Some thoughts are so bizarre, and I'm not even sure where they come from. For instance, I will be on a train, and I will have a thought that I will start licking the dirty passenger window. Or when I clean my pet's drinking water I have a thought that I will drink the soiled water. These thoughts really bother me because I feel an impulse or strong feeling like I am going to do them. It's like I am pushing myself not to react.

I broke a glass in the kitchen and cleaned it up. But now I am having thoughts that shards of glass are everywhere. I know it is ridiculous, but yesterday I threw out an unopened container of pudding that has been in my fridge because I had the thought there could be glass in it. I am losing it, aren't I?

Sometimes for no reason while I am driving, I get the thought that I might have hit someone and that person is lying dying in the road. I try to think back if I heard or felt anything, but I just can't be sure. It takes everything I have got not to turn around and go back over the route I just traveled. I tell myself it is just a thought and that there is no evidence, but I still keep doubting myself.

Mental Checking

This occurs alongside the feeling that something just doesn't seem right and that you need to check that out.

While I am reading, I have these thoughts that I am not actually understanding what I am reading, so I have to go back and repeat the sentence to see if I really understood it. It makes reading excruciating and slow, and sometimes I just give up. I think there is something wrong with my reading comprehension.

After I leave a phone conversation, I often have the thought that I might have insulted someone without realizing it, and then, even if I know it isn't true, I have to go back and reconstruct the entire conversation sentence by sentence and try to remember the exact tone of voice to make sure that everything is okay. Then I start having even more thoughts that something subtle was wrong, and I can't figure out exactly what happened.

Doubts About Relationships

You fear that your intrusive doubting thought is an indication of something being or going wrong, despite little evidence to the contrary.

I am full of anxiety about my relationship. I have become obsessed with the question of whether I love my partner for the right reasons. I am overcome with fear even though I know I love my partner, but my brain is going crazy. I shake and just want to cry. I have read about ROCD (relationship obsessive compulsive disorder). Is this a real thing?

I honestly believe that my husband is faithful to me, but I keep thinking that I do not actually know what he is doing for many hours of each day. I try to keep myself from checking his pockets, his cell phone, and his e-mail, and from asking him for details of his day when I know the reason I am doing this is to make sure he is not having an affair. If his eyes follow a pretty woman or he is nice to a waitress, I am flooded with doubts and ask myself stupid questions like "Does he actually know her?" and

"Why is he being so pleasant?" I am driving myself and him nuts.

Scrupulous Thoughts

These involve judgments about yourself or others in action, intention, or character. This category includes both religious and nonreligious preoccupation with your thoughts about right and wrong and judging your or someone else's attempts to be totally pure, good, kind, fair, and giving.

My younger sister just got engaged. I tell her I am happy for her and say all the right things, but secretly I am really jealous of her and can't help thinking that I should be the first one to get engaged. I am such a bad person; I want to be generous, but these jealous thoughts won't go away

When I say my prayers, I feel as if I am just saying them automatically, and I think I do not have a feeling of worship, just the words.

I have such privilege, and I know I am not doing enough for poor people. I give to charities and at church, but I can never tell how much to give—I think I am never giving enough. I know I am not Mother Teresa, but I am always thinking that I am selfish if I buy something I don't need and that I should just give away all my money. I always feel guilty if I overeat; someone else is starving, and I am getting second helpings. It makes it hard to enjoy anything.

Sexual-Orientation and Sexual-Identity Thoughts

These types of intrusive thoughts center around the fear that you might possibly be living a life that is different from your true sexual identity or orientation. Your thoughts are not like those of people who are truly trying to explore their sexuality. They are filled with terror, not curiosity, alongside an urgent need to know and to know for sure. Perhaps you are upset by your thoughts, even if you believe that it is okay to be straight or gay, but that does nothing to calm your fears. You are bewildered by these thoughts because they just don't fit with what you know about yourself. These thoughts preoccupy you.

What If I'm Really Gay?

Often this begins with a sudden whoosh of an upsetting thought that seems contrary to what you have always assumed about yourself.

I am having a terrible time thinking that I am attracted to my roommate. He is straight, I thought I was too, I have a girlfriend I love, but I feel like I just am going to ruin our friendship by confessing I am having these feelings, and then he will never be comfortable with me again. I keep testing myself to see if I really am attracted to him. I even tried to look at gay porn to see if I liked it, but that did not settle anything for me. That made it even worse. I can't get this out of my mind.

I married my boyfriend, and he is my best friend, but last year I suddenly started having thoughts that I didn't love him, which were a l l - c o n s u m i n g and anxiety-provoking. Then during an anxious time, the thought that maybe I'm a lesbian popped in my head, and that has been the most distressing. I was able to get rid of it for short periods of time, but now it's stuck. It is not that I think being a lesbian is wrong or bad.

What If I'm Really Straight?

These thoughts are not part of a natural process of self-discovery. They feel different from regular thoughts.

I am gay, I have been with the same boyfriend for thirteen years, and sometimes he just turns me off. People say this is normal, but then I wonder if maybe all these years I have just been fooling myself that I am gay because I am too much of a loser to try to date women. Then I start thinking, What if I am attracted to this woman, and how could I do that to Steve? I mean, I do like women. Then I am plagued by doubts, and I start testing myself. I even watched some straight porn to see if I got aroused and who I watched more, the man or the woman. What a waste of time, but I keep worrying about it. Why is this suddenly an issue after all these years?

What If I'm Transgender?

Transgender people have always sensed their gender identities and birth bodies do not match. But an intrusive thought about gender identity can happen to anyone.

I have been reading all these articles about trans-people. Now I have had this repeating feeling that my breasts are bothering me because they are too big. Then I had this frightening thought that if I don't want breasts, I could be a boy trapped in a girl's body and that I was really meant to be a boy. I did some more Internet research, and I am worried this could be me. I can't stop thinking about this no matter how hard I keep telling myself it is silly. But why would I be thinking this?

Intrusive Visual Images

We can think in two different ways. One type of thinking is in the form of words, sort of talking to yourself inside your head. Another way is to have images or pictures in your mind. Although many intrusive thoughts are experienced as disturbing "self-talk," there are a number that are almost exclusively visual images (Brewin et al. 2010). You may have noticed this yourself.

Here are some of the most common kinds of intrusive visual images. Intrusive images can be static pictures or short "videos." They may incorporate actual memories or be completely made up.

Crazy or Humiliating Actions

Many people think they are hallucinating when they have a visual image of themselves doing something crazy or humiliating in a social setting, but they are not. These visual images often happen during socially anxious situations, and they are simply imaginative products of stuck thoughts translated into images instead of words.

I keep having an image of myself vomiting all over myself and other people—you know, like President Bush—whenever I am at a formal event.

Whenever I am being interviewed and whenever I'm at a party, I imagine myself freezing or yelling out something that makes no sense, and people will say, "What is wrong with that woman? She's a crazy lady!"

I don't go to parties because I see myself blanking out and not being able to talk or control myself when people ask me questions.

Sometimes when I meet someone new, I will actually see a little movie of myself poking my finger into that person's eye or suddenly leaping across the room to strangle him or her. And this is even crazier—sometimes I see a dagger hanging in the air in front of me kind of tempting me to take it.

Illness, Dying, and Death Scenes

These disturbing pictures can intrude any time—when you are relaxed, having fun, driving, or anxious about something else.

Sometimes I have a sudden picture of myself bleeding to death from Ebola, and the more I try to not look, the more gruesome the image. I get sick to my stomach.

For no reason, I have a picture myself dead in a coffin except somehow I know I am not really dead, and I am trying to yell to the people at my funeral to get me out.

Sometimes as I am driving over the bridge, I see myself careening over the side and falling toward the water; it is so vivid that I wonder if it is an omen.

Traumatic Memories

Traumatic images and memory intrusions often happen when someone has PTSD, but they can also happen to someone with a sticky mind who is upset by a thought, a memory, or even an imagined image. These may be a sudden reexperiencing, as if the traumatic events are happening again in the present (usually called flashbacks), accompanied by fear or whatever emotion happened at the time. Or they may simply be vivid, fixed visual memories of real things that happened or were imagined at the time of the traumatic experience.

I keep seeing the car coming at me, over and over.

The face of the man who raped me keeps coming into my mind, and I freeze.

I can be anywhere, and suddenly I see myself dropping to the ground when the soldiers came to my door.

I saw the news reports about the plane crash, and now I "see" a horrible scene in the plane as it is falling out of the sky. Everyone is screaming and crying. I know I wasn't there, but I can't stop seeing it.

While flashbacks and traumatic memories are indeed just thoughts and images and are therefore not dangerous in and of themselves, they may be stored in the brain in a different way because of the high impact of the original experience. If there is actually PTSD and not just a sticky mind, there are additional treatment methods not in this book that may be helpful. It may be worth consulting a trauma specialist for help with the other PTSD symptoms that often go along with flashbacks and difficult memories.

Worry

Everyone knows about worry. There is no one who has never experienced the anxiety of an intense worry jag. So, even though worry is universal to human beings, we include worry as one type of unwanted intrusive thought because there are really two types of worry—productive worry and toxic worry (Leahy 2005).

Productive worry is a form of planning: it starts with a problem and comes up with an answer to that problem and an action plan to follow. Plus—and this is important—the solution and action plan then stop the worrying. So, as a very simple example, let's suppose you are driving in your car, look down, and realize that your gas tank is very low. You might worry about running out of gas. But then you come up with a solution in the form of *I'm going to fill up at the gas station down the road.* That action plan seems to solve your problem and stops your worrying.

Toxic worry, on the other hand, involves trying to solve an issue where the outcome is uncertain or unknowable and there is no good answer to form an action plan. So you start to "solve" the problem once and can't seem to come up with any good answer. So the worry returns, and then the entire process continues to repeat. It becomes stuck. Toxic worry starts with a what-if and continues in an endless loop of unsatisfactory "solutions." Attempts to solve the problem in order to reassure yourself fail.

Toxic worry can be about ordinary things like friendships, money, and scheduling—or it can be about highly unlikely things like rare illnesses and catastrophic events. What defines toxic worry is not what the worrying is about, but how the worries behave—they get stuck, repeat, escalate, and preoccupy. They don't subside and take a back seat when no solution can be found. So you are trying to engage in mental problem solving, but all you come up with are other possible negative outcomes (Borkovec et al. 1983). In other words, no matter what False Comfort might say to Worried Voice, no matter how sensible or reassuring or distracting, Worried Voice has something else to come back with that keeps the what-if questions coming.

There are three types of toxic worry: single-topic, multi-topic, and meta-worry (worry about worry).

> **Helpful Fact:** Toxic worry is not defined by the worry topic, but how the worry thoughts behave.

Single-Topic Worrying

Sometimes you can worry about just one thing, going over all the different possibilities and possible outcomes related to that single topic.

I worry about my children every day. When I drop them off at the bus, I worry that they will get into an accident on the school bus. When I hear them cough, I worry that they might have asthma or pneumonia. I'm afraid they might get sick from their inoculations. I don't let them play sports after school because I worry they might get injured. I worry that dental X-rays will hurt them.

Multi-Topic Worrying

Worry can also be expansive and often spreads creatively from one topic to another.

Right now, I'm worried that a mole on my arm is melanoma, and I'm worried about the biopsy results. But then I'm ready to worry about my husband because his PSA (prostate-specific antigen) levels might be going up, and I don't know how I can survive without him. And my daughter is 15½ and about to get her learner's permit. I'm terrified of her being on the road by herself. I worry that all this stress is destroying my immune system. How will my children survive without me?

The world has become such a dangerous place. I am afraid to go in a shopping mall now that terrorists have threatened us. I can get most things online, but I am still worried for my friends who don't watch the news. More and more things worry me—like toxins. How far is this going to go?

I could not sleep last night because I think I may have upset my friend with what I said, but she will never tell me, even if I ask, because she is too polite. Do you think she is angry at me? Now I am worrying about other people I might have offended. It is so easy to offend and not realize it; I haven't heard from another friend for weeks, I wonder if I offended her too.

I have to take a test next week, and I am worried that I won't be able to concentrate, that I will fail the test, and that will make me do poorly in this course, which will affect my ability to get into law school. I have to get into law school. The more I think about it, the more I feel like my whole future is on the line if I don't ace this test. And that makes me worry even more. Now I can't concentrate, and my whole life can go down the tubes.

If you get involved in multiple-thought toxic worry, your thoughts often involve a chain of catastrophic or negative possibilities that seem to force themselves into your awareness. Most people feel that they are uncontrollable.

Meta-Worry (Worry About Worry)

Here, you worry that your worrying will damage your health, indicate that you are an undesirable person, or point to some other negative aspect of yourself.

I read in a magazine that worrying is stress on the immune system and stress can contribute to diabetes and heart disease. I do everything I can to control my worrying because I know it can make me sick. My friends tell me that I am shortening my life with all my worrying. I already do Pilates, and I even drink green tea and pomegranate juice, but they aren't helping. Maybe I should quit my job? It's so stressful!

I'm sick of worrying all the time. I'm such a downer, and I know I've lost friends and boyfriends because of my worrying. People don't want to be with someone like me, and I can't blame them. I always see something that could go wrong, and

I need to make sure everything is just right. I have no joy in my life, and I suck it from everyone around me.

When I can't control my thoughts, I feel like I am going crazy, and I worry about how long I can hold onto my sanity. My cousin has schizophrenia, and they say he started to act strange while he was in college, and it was downhill from there.

When I lie down to sleep, I can't stop the thoughts. I review everything I did that day and look for my mistakes. Or I am planning for tomorrow. Or I have to get up to urinate—or at least I think I do—and I watch the clock. Then I start thinking, Oh no. I only have three or four hours left to sleep, and I have to sleep. If I can't sleep, I will not be able to work tomorrow, then more clock watching and worrying about sleeping tomorrow night.

Not Entirely Unwanted Intrusive Thoughts

Sometimes we find ourselves with uninvited thoughts or imagined scenes that are embarrassing or upsetting, but they seem to help our mind deal with something bothersome or painful, about which there is really nothing to do. They may serve as a diversion in a trapped situation or as a fantasy that makes us feel less helpless. They may be a preoccupation that keeps us from needed concentration, but the content was at least originally invited in.

Revenge

Here is an example of invited thoughts that turn uninvited and intrusive when they are judged dangerous or wrong.

Every time my boss stands in my doorway, I start thinking I am going to blast him for what he said to me last week. I never would of course, but yesterday I started imagining letting the air out of his tires in the parking lot. And then I started asking myself if I would ever lose control and do it.

Bereavement

It is not the images and thoughts of someone who died that are necessarily uninvited. But if you are trying to get over it and move on or if you are worried that you are grieving in an unhealthy way, a struggle ensues.

When I lie down at night, I see my mother's face as I remember her before she was sick, and I can't fall asleep. I am so sad. I look at photographs during the day. I hear her voice talking to me at the oddest times. I think about her constantly.

Love Sickness

Falling in love can be totally obsessive at any age. Feeling unable to keep the thoughts in check can be difficult especially if people around you notice. You can feel like you are losing perspective and becoming out of control.

I am completely obsessed with him. I can't concentrate. I want to know where he is and what he is doing every moment. Everything is dull and boring unless he is by my side. We text all day long. I can't get anything done. This is over the top; I am going to lose my job if I don't stop thinking about him.

Resentment

Sometimes we entertain thoughts we wish we did not, and we enjoy them and try to push them away at the same time.

My friend inherited a lot of money, and she is naturally thin and can eat whatever she wants. The other day she got reprimanded at work, and I have to admit I had the thought, Finally something is not so easy for her! I am ashamed of myself for thinking this.

Not entirely unwanted intrusive thoughts are only a problem if you start struggling with them, if you worry about them and what they mean, or if you judge them as sick or bad. They pass when the emotion that is driving them (anger, grief, early romance, resentment) subsides over time. They are not indications of character or impulses to be resisted: they are your rich imagination at work. No one is free of not entirely unwanted intrusive thoughts. It is only the struggle against them that is problematic

Personal Loss, Failure, or Mistake

There are a number of unwanted intrusive thoughts that center around the theme of past or future mistakes. Your thoughts may be experienced as "irrational" and overblown, but even so, there is the sense that you, in fact, have committed a terrible mistake that might never be undone. This makes you very anxious. You may have something specific in mind, or it may just be a sense that something important slipped your awareness or memory.

When I was working as an attorney, I worked on a case that got a lot of press and we won the case. But now I keep thinking that I never shared a minor detail with the other side, and even though it

was almost twenty years ago, I keep having the thought that if someone found out about this, my reputation could be ruined. I have asked my partner how important this is, and she says it is trivial and to stop worrying about it, but it comes to me at all hours of the day and night.

I keep coming back to the thought that I should never have broken up with that boyfriend, even though he treated me terribly, the relationship seemed doomed, and I was miserable. At least I thought it seemed doomed. But I keep wondering if things could have somehow turned around. I keep trying to remember the moment when I messed it up.

As soon as I submit a paper for publication, I have the thought that my statistical analysis was wrong or I left out a vital piece of data. Or there is something unethical in the research, and I worry about this ruining my career. It keeps me awake at night.

Is it right to make amends for something you aren't sure about? I think I stole ten dollars from a friend in middle school; although to tell you the truth, I am not sure if I did or I made it up. It was thirty-four years ago, but maybe I should apologize or send her the money in case it is true. I try to tell myself it is not important, but the thought keeps coming back, so it must need resolution, right?

If I hadn't lost that money, I could take care of my family better. I am so worried that I won't be able to afford retirement. I push the thoughts away, but it remains the monster in the room.

I lost the girl of my dreams! I can't believe that I let her go, and now I will never find love. I was so stupid, and now it's too late to get her back. I can't stop thinking about this. It makes me so sad.

Somatosensory Intrusions

Some people have intrusive sensations instead of thoughts, but they act the very same way as unwanted thoughts and images. Psychologists sometimes view these sensory intrusions as a form of hyper-awareness OCD. You feel a desire or a need to resist thoughts and observations about sensations. There are some self-help books on obsessive-compulsive disorder that address this issue as well (see, for example, Hershfield, Corboy, and Claiborn 2013).

I have a feeling that I am producing too much saliva. I keep swallowing and swallowing. I check to see if there is more, and there always is; I can't stop, and it is driving me nuts. Now it feels like I have a lump in my throat too.

I am tortured by my underwear. I can't get any to fit right.

When I lie in bed trying to sleep, I feel like I have to pee, even if I just did a few minutes ago. Then I think I won't be able to sleep unless I go again. This can go on for hours and hours.

A friend pointed out to me that she could see the side of her nose if she looked down. Now I can't stop seeing my nose, it feels like it is obstructing my vision, and I hate it. Does anyone else have this?

When I lie down at night, I can hear my heartbeat in my ear. I can't relax. I can't stop counting and listening and worrying about it. I have started getting up over and over to check my blood pressure and pulse. What is wrong with me?

Worried Voice: What is wrong with me that I keep hearing my pulse in my ear? It is so annoying and irritating. And I can't get rid of the idea that it means I have some heart problem.

False Comfort: Don't worry about your heart. You went to the doctor two months ago. Don't think about it. Focus on some other sound, like the sound of the refrigerator in the kitchen.

Worried Voice: But I can't. I try that, and then I think, *What is wrong with me that I can't even distract myself?* I figure that either I have something wrong with my heart or else I get worried that this will never stop—that it might go on forever.

False Comfort: Just stop those negative thoughts. I know you can do that. Maybe if you sing a song to yourself, or keep the TV on, it will drown out the sound of your heartbeat.

Worried Voice: I tried it, and it doesn't work. I keep checking in my mind to see if I can hear my pulse, and then think that I really should check my blood pressure. But I know this is crazy, and so I think what a weird person I am to have this messed-up sort of problem. What kind of person has a problem like this?

Wise Mind: Believe it or not, your ongoing back-and-forth discussion is what keeps you stuck on the sounds. Leave them alone. *Allow them to be.* And checking your pulse and blood pressure keeps you focused on frightening thoughts. Just because you have a thought does not make it a fact. I suggest that you don't distract yourself. And remember that it's not the sound itself, but the way you react to the sound that makes it feel so irritating and dangerous.

Worried Voice: How will allowing it to be there possibly help?

Wise Mind: Give it a try. Clearly your way is not working.

> **Helpful Fact:** Most of your distress is caused not by what you think or feel, but how you feel about and react to what you think or feel.

You have now read about the wide range of unwanted intrusive thoughts. We have provided you with some very specific and explicit examples, and it is not uncommon for readers to experience a spike in anxiety. But be assured that the upset is temporary, and you will find it a small price to pay for the benefits of knowing that you are not alone as well as of having the opportunity to find your own specific type or types of unwanted intrusive thoughts.

Seeing these on the written page will give you some initial relief, no matter what kinds of thoughts have become stuck and repetitive in your mind. And the fact that people with intrusive thoughts like yours have recovered and live normal lives proves that your situation is not as serious, crazy, or hopeless as it may currently feel. In the next chapter, we will address the myths that need debunking, about both thoughts in general and about unwanted intrusive thoughts specifically.

CHAPTER 3

What Thoughts Mean: Myths and Facts

There are nine myths about thoughts in general that contribute to intrusive thoughts becoming stuck. Busting these myths with facts will go a long way toward helping you change your attitude about your mind.

We all have beliefs about thoughts and what they say about us. Many of us believe that what runs through our minds tells a story about the person we are underneath. Some of our ideas about our thoughts might be correct, but we now understand that a lot of common beliefs are false, and these false beliefs can cause a great deal of unhappiness.

Every day, researchers learn more about thinking and what the content of your thoughts say about the sort of person you are. The newest information contradicts some long-held ideas about what thoughts mean and what kinds of thoughts are normal. This chapter debunks the nine major myths about thoughts that contribute to unwanted intrusive thoughts. Since each myth contributes to the tendency to be stuck on unwanted intrusive thoughts, it makes sense for you to consider each one and think about how much you hold onto each myth. There is conclusive evidence from psychological research that each one is false.

Helpful Fact: Busting myths with facts about thoughts will make intrusive thoughts less sticky.

Myth 1: Our Thoughts Are Under Our Control

Many people falsely believe that our thoughts are under our conscious control, and so we should be able to control our thoughts.

Fact: The fact is that many of our thoughts—and some researchers believe that *most* of our thoughts—are not under conscious control. There are times when we welcome this fact. An insight or an inspiration can help solve a problem. Ask a poet or songwriter how she finds lyrics, and she might say it just comes to her. Sometimes a thought just pops up, like a mental tic or hiccup. Ask anyone who practices meditation. We aren't in control of it, and we aren't responsible for it. Thoughts just happen. They wander. They jump around. They don't take orders.

Occasionally it hits you in the face that you can't control your thoughts. Everyone has a wandering mind when listening to boring talks. A noisy room can interrupt your train of thoughts. And when was the last time you thought about an argument at home when speaking to someone at work? How often do you tell yourself to think confident thoughts, only to be aware of self-criticism and worries creeping in?

Just because you can think some thoughts on purpose doesn't mean that you are in control of them. You can't make your thoughts go away at will. You can focus your attention on certain thoughts, but that doesn't mean you have the capacity to make them go away.

Worried Voice: I wish I could control my thoughts, especially when I get a bad thought. I think I am sick.

False Comfort: What you need is some mental discipline. Try harder!

Worried Voice: I'm trying, but I can't seem to do it. I think I'm broken.

Wise Mind: Everyone's mind goes everywhere. It could be interesting to watch. I have no need to stop any of it. Nor do you. Thoughts are just thoughts, and they just happen.

Worried Voice and False Comfort both believe in the myth that control of thoughts, especially disturbing thoughts, is not only possible but necessary for mental health. They are quite wrong. Wise Mind knows better.

Belief in the myth that you are in control of your thoughts leads to the common but unhelpful suggestion that you can replace negative thoughts with positive ones and that this will help you control what you think. The facts indicate that you can deliberately think positive thoughts and distract your attention temporarily from unwanted thoughts to chosen ones. But the thoughts you are trying to replace tend to persist and *usually return even more forcefull* y to your attention. How many times have you tried to push a thought away, only to have it pop right back up?

Myth 2: Our Thoughts Indicate Our Character

Another thought myth is that thoughts speak to our character or underlying intentions and that some people have an underlying dark side that is revealed only in their thoughts.

Fact: We know that thoughts have nothing to do with character. Character is a reflection of how you lead your life. It relates to what you actually choose to do or choose not to do. Thoughts are what pass through your mind. When thoughts just happen, it is not your choice. There is no place for issues of character when there is no chance for choice. A thought is not a fact or a statement about yourself. *Character is about the choices you make in life,* not what pops into your mind.

This myth is often illustrated by elaborate metaphors in popular culture. Most frightening are examples of apparently perfectly nice people being taken over by their dark side, whether it be the metaphor of werewolves, possession, Jekyll and Hyde, or some other way of innocent people turning into killers. Movies such as *The Exorcist, American Psycho,* and *Forbidden Planet* are designed to terrify people into thinking that, no matter how innocent or well-intentioned you are, there might be an evil force inside of you ready to take over. These fantasies fuel the false idea that one's underlying thoughts reveal actual intentions or nature even if disavowed, as if there can be an inner demon that can leap out against your will.

Similarly, movies and books about the breakdown of society, such as *Lord of the Flies, Mad Max,* and other post-apocalyptic nightmares, suggest that our survival instincts can turn us into moral monsters. They all imply that we are precariously civilized. Taking this one step further implies that uncivilized thoughts are the tip of the iceberg and that one's true nature or character may not be what it seems.

Interestingly, often people apply this myth only to themselves and their own thoughts. If a friend relates a wild, repugnant, or nonsensical thought, you are quick to reassure him that minds are capricious, that these thoughts are not meaningful, and that you have not lost respect for him. It's easy to joke about someone else's intrusive thoughts.

Worried Voice: I'm always coming up with perverted thoughts. Even about children. I must be a bad person deep down. It happens all the time.

False Comfort: Don't be silly. We both know you are good. Crowd out the perverted thoughts. Thinking about it could make you doubt yourself.

Worried Voice: I try, but it just keeps happening. I wonder if something bad happened to me that I don't remember, and it is stuck in my unconscious. They say abused people become abusers.

False Comfort: People can overcome their bad thoughts. You just have to stay positive.

In this dialogue, both Worried Voice and False Comfort believe that thoughts indicate character and then struggle to deal with this. They are both falling prey to this myth.

> **Helpful Fact:** Thoughts have nothing to do with character. Only chosen actions do.

Myth 3: Our Thoughts Indicate the Inner Self

This is the belief that thoughts are paths to our inner self, sort of like eyes being windows to the soul. This includes the belief that whatever is in our mind is a reflection of our true thoughts and feelings, no matter how we might protest it is not so. So intrusive thoughts must speak some special, perhaps hidden, truth about us.

Fact: The fact is that *everyone* has passing weird, aggressive, or crazy thoughts. If every thought spoke to underlying character, then 90 percent of people would be weird, aggressive, or crazy. That is because about 90 percent of people acknowledge having intrusive thoughts that they characterize as weird, aggressive, frightening, or crazy. And think about some of the horror movies and TV shows that are so popular these days. Perhaps you are unable to watch them because they trigger too much fear. But remember that these awful, weird, aggressive, and crazy scenarios are thought up by normal, creative people. They are simply writing scripts that other people will want to watch.

An implication of this myth is that weird or nonsensical thoughts might indicate loss of control over your mind or even mental illness. Or, another false implication is that if you have intrusive repugnant thoughts, it could mean that you are a perverted or disgusting person.

People with unwanted aggressive or violent thoughts may become fearful that they are violent or angry *despite having no awareness of these emotions,* and that their true feelings are indicated by these thoughts. They may come to believe not only that they must be bad people at their core, but they may also feel an extra burden to exercise serious control over these thoughts.

We all have mental activity going on outside of awareness, and it is interesting to wonder how certain mental events happen to pop up. But there is no truth to the ideas that blips of intrusive thoughts and images reveal underlying truths and that thoughts reveal motives, feelings, and intentions that are deeply meaningful or contain messages that need to be addressed *when they differ from conscious thoughts, feeling, and intentions.*

Myth 4: The Unconscious Mind Can Affect Actions

This is the belief that our unconscious mind is a powerful force that directs our thoughts and behaviors, sometimes operating in the dark and against our conscious minds and will. So there is a possibility that unconscious forces could come leaping out against our wishes and lead us to do something impulsively angry, violent, or mean—even though we don't actually want to.

Fact: Analyzing the meaning of *Freudian slips* and automatic associations—including the content of dreams—are popular ways of trying to understand the complex workings of the unconscious mind. But the momentary thought of dropping your baby certainly does not reveal any unconscious wish to do harm. And the sudden thought that you could jump off the balcony because the railing is low does not reveal hidden unconscious suicidal wishes.

Worried Voice: Every day I take the train to work, and every day I have the thought that I could push someone under the train. What does it mean about me that I have such bad thoughts? Maybe my unconscious mind will make me do it.

False Comfort: Tell yourself that you would never do anything violent. Don't let those thoughts take over. Distract yourself, and think about something else. Pray for relief.

Worried Voice: I try, but I keep on having the thoughts.

Here False Comfort is trying hard to reassure Worried Voice and offers *coping skills* to handle the disturbing thoughts. While coping skills might provide temporary relief, they don't work for long. Unfortunately, they both believe this myth, that such thoughts are meaningful bits of the unconscious mind and require a response.

Another example of this myth is believing that thoughts of doubt are messages, signals, or warnings from the wiser more perceptive unconscious. Some of you may be plagued by doubts about a decision and then believe it means that you made a mistake, and therefore, there is some important issue you need to address. This myth suggests that a doubting thought is a message from your unconscious that repeats itself because it is telling you to reconsider what you did or what you plan to do.

But it is simply not true that feared thoughts are fueled by underlying wishes or are warnings that should be heeded. There is an old assumption, sometimes stated in the form "The wish is father to the fear," suggesting that your fear of doing something terrible is caused by your desire to do it. This is a myth with nothing to support it. It does only one thing: it contributes to the fears of people with unwanted intrusive thoughts.

Myth 5: Thinking Something Makes It Likely to Happen

Believing that thinking something somehow makes that thing more likely to happen or makes it more true is the basis of this myth. Many people don't like the idea of negative thoughts because they believe that having negative thoughts means that more negative things will happen. Some people believe that negative attracts negative and that positive attracts positive.

Fact: This is a complete misunderstanding of what is known about thoughts. Psychologists call this myth *thought-action fusion* (Rachman 1993, Salkovskis 1985) or magical thinking. The fact is that a thought is not a message about what is going to happen. Similarly, a thought is not a prediction or a warning of an awful action or occurrence in the future. Thoughts do not warn of plane crashes, automobile accidents, or natural disasters. Premonition is a feeling that comes with a thought; it is not an accurate reading of the future. We tend to remember the rare premonitions that come true and forget all the many other doubts and feelings that passed without coming true.

Even more importantly, your thoughts cannot make unwanted actions or events happen. *Thoughts do not change probabilities in the real world.* Thoughts do not move objects, nor can they hurt people. Additionally, thoughts are not aspects of your unconscious that might become uncaged and leap up and take control if you don't remain vigilant. Thinking that someone might die will not make him more likely to die; a wandering thought about what it would be like to be unfaithful to a partner does not make you seek an affair; a sudden fearful thought does not make real danger or disaster any more likely. Please don't confuse thoughts with facts. A fact can be true, or it can be false. A thought is just a thought. Thoughts are often our guesses about the world around us and the way it seems to operate. Thoughts themselves have no effect on the world.

> **Helpful Fact:** Thoughts do not change probabilities in the real world.

But some of you might be thinking, *But if I have negative thoughts, won't I be doing more negative things?*

Well, to some extent that is true. Sometimes your mood and motivation can change in response to your thoughts and beliefs. Here's an example: If you believe that something is going to be very frightening, then you will approach that with more trepidation, and you might even decide to stay away from it because you aren't sure you will be able to handle the fear. And if you think that your boss is going to give you a really hard time about leaving early on Tuesday to see your son's soccer final, you might decide to call in sick that day or maybe just forgo the game. In other words, sometimes our beliefs and thoughts can influence what we *choose* to do. But this is very different from the false believe that thinking about something influences the chances of it occurring.

Myth 6: Thinking Something Makes It Unlikely to Happen

Myth 6 is almost the exact opposite of myth 5. Specifically, it is that thinking something will make it *less* likely to happen or make it *less* true. You may believe that thinking about a person you care for—specifically worrying about someone—is a way of protecting that person, showing love and loyalty, and keeping bad things from happening. Staying involved with worry thoughts seems like a way of remaining vigilant—and somehow more prepared—for danger.

Fact: Once again, thoughts do not change probabilities in the real world. While worrying about someone might make you *feel* like you are doing something to protect him or her, in reality you are only training your brain to reinforce a cycle of ongoing worry. Remember that feelings are not facts. Feeling that you need to stay engaged by constantly thinking about someone is falling for the false alarms of anxiety.

Myth 7: Only Sick People Have Intrusive Thoughts

This refers to the mistaken belief that only disturbed people have intrusive or weird thoughts.

Fact: The fact is that no one is entirely free of weird, repugnant, and disturbing passing thoughts. This means that just about everyone you know, including your friends, your work colleagues, your teachers, and your doctors have also experienced intrusive thoughts. In fact, Mother Teresa had unwanted intrusive thoughts (Teresa

2009). So, most probably, does your favorite celebrity and your pastor.

The big difference is that just about everyone has *passing* intrusive thoughts. Your intrusive thoughts feel very different because they are repeated and sometimes become stuck. This makes them feel particularly disturbing, like they are the product of a disturbed mind. But the stickiness of these thoughts has nothing at all to do with your character or your value as a human being. And it certainly has nothing to do with being a disturbed person. The stickiness has a lot to do with how you think and feel about these thoughts and the methods and intensity you are using to try to rid yourself of them.

In chapter 5, we will show you how a passing intrusive thought—which everyone has—becomes a stuck and unwanted intrusive thought through no fault, personality defect, or mental illness of your own.

Myth 8: Every Thought Is Worth Thinking

Myth 8 is that every thought is worth thinking about, so it makes sense to and it is worthwhile to explore the content of any thought that crosses your mind or comes to your attention.

Fact: The fact is that you, like cable TV, have many different channels of thought going through your mind at the same time. It is impossible to think about them all, and some of your channels are just full of junk (like maybe the infomercial channel or the local high school announcements). Not all are worthwhile to think about. Imagine that you are listening to your radio and something went wrong, so instead of listening to one station at a time, you were listening to two, three, five, or ten at once. One channel might be great music that you want to hear; another might be an absorbing discussion. Others might be a boring repeat newscast, a song that you hate, and a story that you have heard a hundred times before. Without giving it much thought, you would work to focus on the things that seemed interesting and let the other channels pass you by.

Similarly, you have more than one "thought channel" going through your mind. Mostly you pick and choose what to focus on without putting in very much effort. Some thoughts just seem more interesting to pursue than others. But when an intrusive thought pops up—no matter what the content—if you believe that all thoughts are worth thinking about (i.e., if you believe that there are no junk channels of the mind), you might choose to focus on that one thought and grant it meaning and attention it does not deserve. Your attention may be hijacked by junk. This is especially true if you believe the intrusive thought is *really* important or if you believe that you have been issued a message or a signal or a warning sign. In cases like this, you can get stuck, and the thought will keep recycling through your mind, asking for your attention.

In truth, all minds are chock full of junk thoughts not worth taking seriously. If we wander into junk thoughts and they are not granted meaning, they just pass on by.

Helpful Fact: Your attention may be hijacked by junk.

Chapter 7 explains how to remain more focused on the natural flow of your thoughts. We will show you how it is possible to care so little about intrusive thoughts that they recede into the background and do not need your attention at all.

Worried Voice: I am trying to study, and all I can think about is whether or not I should marry my boyfriend.

False Comfort: You have only known each other a few weeks. Don't think about that now. You have to study.

Worried Voice: Yes, I know, but I feel like I should think about it because I had the thought that he will ask me.

False Comfort: Do you think that means he really will ask you?

Worried Voice: Well, sort of. I should be prepared; shouldn't I? What if he does ask me? I really need to be studying. If I do poorly on the exam tomorrow, I could lose my scholarship.

False Comfort: Remember what you put yourself through with the last guy?

Worried Voice: But this time it feels like a real issue.

Wise Mind: Hey guys, you are both listening to the junk channel. Just because it popped into your mind does not mean it requires your attention. Just because someone lobs a football at you does not mean you have to catch it. Junk channels lob junk at us all the time.

Myth 9: Thoughts That Repeat Are Important

You may believe that thoughts that repeat must be important. After all, it would seem, if a thought were not important, it would just fly out of our mind and be forgotten. The fact that the thought keeps recurring must mean that it is significant.

Fact: The fact is that the importance of a thought has very little to do with how much it repeats. Actually, thoughts tend to repeat if they are resisted or pushed away. So if you have a repeating thought that you are resisting, that same thought will start to fade away when you stop trying to resist it. Any thought that you attempt to squish is more likely to keep repeating, like *Don't think about that itchy spot, Stop rerunning that commercial jingle through your mind,* or *Stop noticing the piece of food in her teeth.*

Remember the theme that "what you resist persists" and the carrot exercise in chapter 1? This is actually how your brain works. When we invest energy in any thought, it builds up the neural connections and makes the thought more likely to happen (Pittman and Karle 2015). This works with any thought; it has nothing to do with the importance of it. The simple fact is that your attempts to keep certain thoughts from coming into your mind is what makes them come round again and feel stuck. One example of this is what happens when you try to stop thinking when falling asleep. Everyone has the experience of watching thoughts amplify, elaborate, and repeat the harder we try to banish them and attempt to "stop thinking." We have to be willing to let the mind wander and not fight with it in order to fall asleep naturally.

Helpful Fact: Thoughts that repeat are stuck, not important.

We hope that now you have a better understanding of some of the common myths and misconceptions about the way thoughts work in people's minds. You are therefore better prepared to understand the unwanted intrusive thoughts that currently upset you, how they got stuck, and how to relate to them in a different way. They do not mean what you think they mean, there is no reason to fear them, and they won't go away by resisting them.

Believing even some of these myths can be responsible for ordinary intrusive thoughts becoming stuck. Knowing the facts behind these nine common myths will make intrusive thoughts less likely to stick. Now that we've busted the myths, in the next chapter we will answer some of the common questions that people often ask.

CHAPTER 4

Unwanted Intrusive Thoughts Q and A

So far we have talked about thoughts in general and described the varieties of unwanted intrusive thoughts. We have introduced you to the way that Worried Voice and False Comfort struggle with each other over thoughts, and how Wise Mind can offer a way out of this struggle. Still, you—like most people—may have very specific questions about issues that are particularly bothersome. And you may not be able to ask these questions of others as you are afraid of or ashamed of revealing these struggles. Here are straightforward, specific answers to the questions our patients most frequently ask. Remember that anxiety loves ignorance, and the more facts you know about stuck thoughts, the better equipped you will be to deal with them. Some of these specific answers review topics we have introduced in earlier chapters.

Does thinking about hurting my children mean that "deep down" I harbor anger and aggression?

No. This idea was probably started by the old psychoanalytic belief that fearful thoughts are related to unconscious wishes. This notion was quite popular in the 1950s and earlier, and there are plenty of references about this in traditional psychoanalytic literature. You may have heard some variation of this idea, and maybe you have grown to accept it as true. Perhaps a past therapist has implied this to you.

However, it is now clear that that there isn't one iota of truth to this. This idea is particularly disturbing because it has generated so much misery and guilt in people who have absolutely no reason to feel that way. Unfortunately, there are still a number of psychotherapists who believe it to be true. There are therapists who may try to focus on your wishes in order to uncover denied unconscious feelings as a way to *cure* your intrusive thoughts.

Worse still, some therapists erroneously believe that your thoughts are an indication that you might actually do something harmful to your children. So you are encouraged to understand and "come to terms" with your thoughts, which actually make them even stickier!

Remember that *sticky thoughts are the opposite of wishes.* They become sticky and intrusive precisely because you reject them and fight with them. They are not pleasurable fantasies. They are not unconscious desires. They do not indicate truths about you that need to be explored.

On the other hand, it is entirely normal to sometimes feel loving feelings and sometimes angry feelings toward your children, as well as a full range of emotions that includes guilt, resentment, frustration, and pride. This is normal and part of the emotional life of every parent. Remember that we are talking about intrusive, bizarre, unwelcome thoughts and the horrified feelings that go with them. These are fundamentally different from actions you choose to make, the normal ebb and flow of emotions, and real-life behaviors.

I have unwanted intrusive thoughts of hurting or sexually abusing children. Could I be a child molester or a secret pedophile?

No. And let us be clear: we are not talking about people who are, in fact, very angry and have a history of acting violently or abusively when they are angry or intoxicated. We are also not talking about people who get pleasure out of imagining or having sexual contact with children. Instead, we are talking about violent and sexual thoughts that make no sense to you, that seem alien and against your nature. They feel offensive and horrific, as well as frightening. They seem to come out of nowhere and redirect your attention. You might avoid contact with children because of them, and we hope that you stop doing that. You are not dangerous, and children do not need protection from you. Remember that your anxiety is maintained and reinforced by avoidance.

Why do some of my thoughts feel like impulses?

Even though unwanted intrusive thoughts are signs of overcontrol and not impulsivity, you may actually feel that you have to put a lot of effort to keep yourself from acting on the thoughts. *This is an illusion.* They feel like impulses even though they are not.

You are actually feeling the effects of *anxious thinking,* which is an altered state of awareness. Once your brain sends out an anxiety alarm signal, your perception of many things becomes markedly different. One very consistent change is what psychologists call *thought-action fusion:* when the line between thoughts and actions becomes fuzzy and indistinct. Ordinarily, the differences between thoughts and actions are quite clear, and thoughts are a safe way to rehearse actions without consequences. But when you are anxious, this difference seems to fade away. When you fight hard to avoid a thought, anxiety will skyrocket, and so will your perception of the profound differences between private thoughts, on the one hand, and actions in the real world that have real consequences, on the other. But even if your perception has become distorted by anxiety, it does not mean that the thought is actually an impulse or has any more ability to make you do anything you do not choose to do. A more comprehensive explanation of how the brain sends out false alarms is presented in chapter 5.

But I get so scared; the fight to control myself feels so real. Why?

Another reason why thoughts can feel like impulses is because of the fear the thought provokes. Here is how it works: When we are startled or surprised, or when something happens that tricks us into thinking there is danger, the alarm system part of our brain called the amygdala sends out a danger signal. It instantly makes many things happen in the body that enable us to run away or fight if there were a real danger. You may know this reaction as the fight-or-flight response. This happens automatically, whether the alarm is false or indicates a true danger. The amygdala is not very smart and cannot judge true danger from a false alarm. It just responds to a trigger—real or imagined—with the only thing it can do. It sends out an alarm. If we are startled by a thought and our amygdala automatically sends out such a danger signal, then we react emotionally as if there is danger. The sensations in our body make the thought seem dangerous, impulsive, or important. We discuss this further in chapter 5.

But our brain has a second mechanism located in the higher brain or cortex that has the capacity to say, "Wait a minute—this is just a thought." The cortex is where we think, reason, and judge. The problem is that the message from the higher brain gets there about a half of a second after the first automatic alarm has sounded. So you are feeling like you are in danger, even before your higher brain has the chance to step in. Our trio illustrates how this goes.

Worried Voice: I just felt like I was going to jump up and shout something profane in church. It took everything I had to hold back.

False Comfort: Maybe you should listen to the radio in church to keep you distracted; you sure wouldn't want to do that.

Worried Voice: This is crazy. You wouldn't believe what I was about to shout. I can't even say it.

False Comfort: These impulses are just horrible! Maybe you should stay home and listen to the church service on the radio. If you have to blurt something out, at least no one will know.

Wise Mind: It feels like an impulse, but it is actually an unwanted intrusive thought, not an impulse. The more you fight it, the stronger it feels, right? So try to act as if it doesn't even matter, because it really doesn't.

Think of Worried Voice as representing a false danger signal from the amygdala. False Comfort falls for the trick and tries to figure out what to do about it, as if the danger is real. It is Wise Mind who knows it is a false alarm and that no response is needed.

Why do I have to fight these thoughts all the time?

Here is the really great news: you don't! That's right. Not only do you not have to fight these thoughts, but fighting the thoughts is a major reason why they become stuck and cause so much psychological misery in the first place.

Remember, you try to block the thoughts because their message feels so unacceptable. And as you continue to fight, they become more persistent and more anxiety-arousing. (This is the ironic process once again.)

What is wrong with me?

What is wrong with you is that you have unwanted intrusive thoughts—nothing more and nothing less. Psychologists know that about nine out of ten people experience intrusive thoughts at least occasionally. So you are one of the nine out of ten. What has gone wrong in your situation is that you have taken your thoughts too seriously and believed that the content of your thoughts meant something important about the person you are or the sort of behaviors that you might commit.

I try to avoid things that trigger my thoughts, but some things are unavoidable. What can I do?

You can try to avoid your avoidance. Reading about violent acts might make you have thoughts about violent actions. Or hearing a radio program about a suicide may provoke unwanted images. But this is unrelated to your behavior. In fact, as we show in chapter 8, deliberately provoking these harmless but upsetting thoughts is part of the treatment. It takes the power away from the thoughts when you no longer have to try to avoid or control then

Thoughts don't *cause* any type of behavior. The facts are that at any given time, you are having a wide range of thoughts on a number of topics. Your brain is broadband, although you might not be aware of most of the channels that are playing.

What you do, however, is *choose* your actions, based on your will, your mood, your preferences, and the type of person you are. The suffering over your thoughts actually lies in the way you evaluate them and react to them, not the content of the thoughts themselves. Trying hard to avoid the thoughts will prevent you from learning this.

I was diagnosed with OCD. Is this a part of that?

Yes, it very well might be a part of the issue. There is evidence that a significant number of people who suffer from unwanted intrusive thoughts are also affected by OCD. And there are some good reasons why this is true.

People with OCD experience obsessions, which are thoughts that arrive with a whoosh of emotion, feel dangerous or unacceptable, cause considerable distress, and are accompanied by a strong need to be neutralized or banished. Obsessions are one kind of repeating unwanted intrusive thoughts. There is an OCD cycle that consists of unwanted thoughts that raise anxiety and continuous attempts to lower anxiety by means of compulsions. The compulsions in OCD may be obvious behavioral rituals that feel driven—like washing, checking, ordering, and counting. But there are also compulsions that are entirely in the mind and consist of giving oneself repeated reassurances or ways to discount, undo, or avoid the obsessive thoughts. People with OCD give their thoughts more power than they deserve. If you have OCD, you probably have the tendency to feel very uncomfortable with uncertainty. And, you may have noticed something about Worried Voice and False Comfort. Worried Voice is the one with unwanted intrusive thoughts, many of which are technically obsessions. And False Comfort is the one who tries unsuccessfully to calm Worried Voice down or make Worried Voice stop thinking. Many of the things False Comfort suggests are actually forms of compulsions.

Do people go crazy when thoughts get stuck? Or does this mean that I am already crazy?

Of course not! People probably get the erroneous idea that they can go crazy from how miserable stuck thoughts can make them because they don't understand what is happening. Stuck thoughts do not drive people to psychosis, and having a stuck thought certainly does not mean that someone is crazy.

However, unwanted intrusive thoughts can be so persistent, so anxiety producing, so frustrating, and so shameful that people sometimes say that their thoughts are "driving them crazy." Of course, the phrase here means the same as, for example, when your children are annoying, frustrating, and unwilling to listen to you, and you tell them that they are "driving you crazy." In this case, the phrase means that your kids are getting you frustrated, being uncooperative, and requiring a lot of your energy to keep them in line. (Sounds a lot like unwanted intrusive thoughts, doesn't it?)

Plus, the content of some intrusive thoughts can seem so bizarre (e.g., thinking that you might drink the dog's stale water rather than spilling it out) that you might wonder if these "crazy" thoughts mean that you are, indeed, going crazy. But please remember that stuck thoughts have nothing to do with psychosis, and you know that odd, weird, and crazy-sounding stuck thoughts are just that—odd, weird, and crazy-sounding.

What are the root causes of this problem?

The real problem here is the question because the question is based on false assumptions.

Here is an example: How would you respond to someone who asked you for the best method of bloodletting to cure a person of their fever? You would, of course, say that bloodletting isn't a way to cure a fever. There was a time in the past when people erroneously believed it to cure people. But that was five hundred years ago. So answering the question would just contribute to that old myth.

In the same way, talking about root causes in this context also contributes to an old myth about human emotions. When you think of a root cause, you probably get an image of digging down deep and pulling out every single bit of the problem so that it is eliminated or extinguished from your psyche. This concept was widely accepted fifty years ago, but now we know that this is not how our minds and brains work.

Instead, we now know that most psychological issues are a complicated interaction of what you inherit (genetics), plus maturational processes that go on throughout your life, plus your own personal history, which can include the way you were raised, the important events that occur, the stresses you encounter, and more. More importantly, we now know that determining the historical factors that contribute to unwanted intrusive thoughts are absolutely no help in getting rid of them.

That's right. Learning about *why* you have intrusive thoughts will not help you stop them nor reduce your distress. However, learning *how* you inadvertently keep intrusive thoughts going and *what* you can do to change this will be significant steps toward recovery. In other words, we need to keep our focus on the hows and the whats, and less on the whys.

I honestly and genuinely love life and like the life I'm leading. So why do I have these persistent thoughts about suicide?

Remember that unwanted intrusive thoughts get stuck precisely because you don't want them or agree with them. In the same way that gentle people are offended by and fight with, and therefore end up accidentally getting stuck on, violent thoughts, people who value their lives also accidentally reinforce thoughts they don't agree with. Believe it or not, the momentary idea of killing oneself crosses ordinary people's minds at random moments. Here are examples: *That knife could do real damage—could I slice myself up? Imagine if I just jumped off this ledge. What if I suddenly just yanked the steering wheel and careened into ongoing traffic? If Robin Williams hung himself, could I impulsively do the same?*

Most people pay no attention to such passing thoughts, and the thoughts pass right on. But if you are anxious or worried about yourself, or feel extremely responsible for the care of someone else, and you think such a thought must be attended to, then harmless thoughts like these may suddenly feel threatening or abnormal. This sets up a struggle to resist the thoughts, and this is why they persist.

So it is quite possible for someone who is neither suicidal, depressed, nor crazy to have so-called suicidal thoughts. We prefer to call them unwanted intrusive thoughts instead of suicidal thoughts because that is all they are.

My therapist told me about thought-stopping. Why doesn't it work? What about distraction? The thoughts just come back. I also have tried to meditate, to find a peaceful place, and to not have these thoughts, but I can't do that either.

Like most professionals, your therapist is probably not a specialist in this particular problem and can't keep up with all the latest findings about how your brain works and how to help you recover from unwanted intrusive thoughts. Most of the so-called anxiety management techniques and coping skills that have been popular in the past just aren't helpful for people with intrusive thoughts.

Thought-stopping doesn't work for one huge reason: it's the opposite of what you should be doing. Thought-stopping asks you to do exactly the wrong thing. Using thought-stopping to control intrusive thoughts is something like this: "Okay, you have been trying without success to keep these thoughts out of your mind. In fact, your efforts are a big part of the reason why your thoughts are stuck. So you are now going to try yet another way to stop your thoughts—this time you are going to banish them with thought-stopping." It didn't work in the past, it isn't working in the present, so why in the world would anyone think that it will work if you now try it this way? The answer: it won't. It doesn't work, it has never worked, and it won't work in the future. You are probably doing your thought-stopping exercises just like you were told. The problem isn't you—the problem is that the approach is wrong.

The key is not to try harder to stop thoughts; it is in changing your relationship with the thoughts and your beliefs about them.

Then, they don't need to be stopped and are no longer fed the energy that maintains them.

The same can be said for distraction techniques. Here is the issue with them: When you try to distract yourself from intrusive thoughts, you are reinforcing the idea that you need to keep away from them. That implies that they are somehow dangerous and might lead to something no good. That is the wrong way to look at them. Furthermore, when you distract yourself, although it may help temporarily, you devote a portion of your mind to barring the door and scanning the mind to make sure they don't return. And it is the high-alert, internal monitor that actually invites them back. It is much more helpful—and much more consistent with what we now know about thoughts—to pay attention to the fact that intrusive thoughts may feel terrible but aren't dangerous. So, instead of learning how to distract yourself from the thoughts, your goal is to learn how to reduce the distress they trigger. Thoughts that don't matter have no power.

It is also not possible to meditate away or to intentionally clear the mind of unwanted intrusive thoughts using meditation. A mindful *attitude* (nonjudgmental, curious, self-observational) is certainly part of the solution, but using meditation as a technique for banishing thoughts will not be effective. A regular practice of meditation can—like exercise—be helpful in many ways, but it is not a technique for conquering thoughts.

How can it be that the content of my thoughts is irrelevant? That seems impossible.

We know how odd this sounds, but the fact is that the content of your thoughts is quite important most of the time, yet entirely irrelevant at other times. You will learn how to distinguish regular thoughts from seemingly important unwanted intrusive stuck thoughts. You will learn how to use the way a thought *feels* and *acts* as a method of distinguishing between thoughts worth thinking about and meaningless thoughts that have become stuck. You will learn not to rely on the content of the thought—what the thought *seems* to be about—at all.

It is also important to understand that everyone has intrusive thoughts not worth thinking about. In fact, a great deal of everyone's wandering mind is made up of uninteresting passing observations, reactions, musings, bits and pieces of memories, conditioned associations, and planning. Some of the thinking seems to be what we are deliberately trying to focus on or think about, but a great deal of it is just mental wandering. Sometimes a thought from one part of the mind (we like to call them channels) intrudes into another and temporarily diverts our attention. All of this is normal. Usually, if we do not focus on the content of the intrusion, it passes because it is simply not worth thinking about. But if one of these intrusive thoughts becomes a stuck, repeating, unwanted, rejected, resisted thought, then suddenly the content *falsely* appears to be important.

In the next chapter, we provide you with another perspective on the most bewildering and upsetting issues you face: why these thoughts are so persistent, why they feel like impulses, and why they engender such great anxiety and guilt. We are going take a neurological perspective and explain what happens to your brain and mind when you have an unwanted intrusive thought, showing why much of what happens lies outside of your control and why your efforts can so easily backfire.

CHAPTER 5

How the Brain Creates Unwanted Intrusive Thoughts

Imagine—without any warning at all—a friend jumps behind you and yells, "Boo!" You would probably jump or be startled, and experience a whoosh of fright. And then, after you realized that there was nothing to really fear, the shakes and rapid heartbeat would stop and you would start to calm down. After a few minutes, it would be as if it didn't happen.

This chapter talks about what happens in the brain when you get frightened like this and how you calm down. In addition, we explain what happens in your brain when you become frightened and *don't* calm down right away. This will help you understand why your best efforts to calm yourself haven't been nearly as effective as you would like.

The Neurology of Anxious Arousal

Let's take a closer look at the neurological engine that keeps unwanted intrusive thoughts going. There is an understandable reason why your brain tells you these thoughts are dangerous and why the thoughts can sometimes feel so much like impulses.

There was a time—not long ago, unfortunately—when people with unwanted intrusive thoughts were called weak, crazy, or out of control, or said to be lacking willpower. Now we know it is nothing of the sort, but your brain has inadvertently been programmed to keep these thoughts going. And the best news is that we know how to *rewire* your brain to end them.

The part of your brain that was originally designed to keep you safe during times of danger can become confused and misdirected. It can become so befuddled, in fact, that it can start to misidentify safe things as dangerous. We call this anxiety—when you react to and worry about something quite safe as if it is objectively dangerous. When your brain inadvertently reacts to thoughts as if they were dangerous, it sets the stage for unwanted intrusive thoughts to take hold. As we have shown in earlier chapters, thoughts themselves are never dangerous—they are just thoughts. But the brain can become programmed to fear thoughts anyway. And this can happen to anyone.

We know that the brain learns as a result of experiences. Fearful experiences are remembered and stored in particularly vivid ways. When fearful pathways are triggered frequently, they become automatic. (Neurologists like to say, "Nerves that fire together, wire together.") Just as we associate two things together, like "up and down" and "left and right," a well-worn pathway in the brain associates two things that follow each other, and they become connected (what psychologists call "conditioned"). If a thought is followed by an anxious experience, the pathway from thought to fear gets established. When this happens repeatedly, your brain becomes conditioned to react anxiously and automatically to that thought. This sets up the conditions for unwanted intrusive thoughts to take hold.

The good news, however, is that scientists have recently learned that it is far easier for your brain to learn new pathways than previously thought and that new reactions can overtake old ones. In other words, don't believe the adage that you can't teach old dogs new tricks! The age of the dog is irrelevant—*any* brain can learn. Getting over unwanted intrusive thoughts involves creating new pathways that are not fearful. This chapter lays the groundwork for understanding how this happens.

The Alarm Response

To understand how unwanted intrusive thoughts work, we start with the alarm response that is built into everyone's brain. This response is sometimes called the stress response, the fight-or-flight response, or—most accurately—the fight, flight, or freeze response. It sets up your body to go through a whole series of arousals—all of which are helpful when you are in danger. These responses include release of adrenaline, increased heart rate, changes in breathing, hypervigilance to possible danger, tunnel vision, and a host of other perceptual changes. You feel this as a whoosh of fear or terror. The alarm response is centered in the amygdala, which consists of two walnut-sized structures in your brain. The amygdala can be either on or off: it either triggers the alarm response or it doesn't. The alarm response is wordless—think of it like a clanging danger-warning bell. There are no partial responses or other subtleties.

Because it is designed to alert you to danger, your amygdala is triggered by just the *merest hint* of a *possible* danger. Its job is to protect you—not to keep you comfortable—so it would rather set off a thousand false alarms and create a thousand whooshes of fear when there is no problem at all than miss one that is real. It was originally designed for primitive survival. Clanging the alarm when there is no danger is called a *false positive.* Remaining silent when there is a real danger is a *false negative.* Your amygdala sends out many, many false positive responses because it never wants to risk a false negative.

In situations of real danger, such as a car swerving toward you on the highway or a falling rock, the rapid reaction time, muscle strength, and increased blood circulation that are part of your alarm system serve you well. The immediate change in your breathing is what you need for emergency sprinting. Even sweating helps air-condition you as you heat up while running. Your amygdala is designed to save your life, and so it responds very rapidly to protect you from threats.

Figure 1 shows the whoosh of fear people feel when the amygdala is triggered. The trigger might be the car coming toward you or the sudden sound of your friend yelling "Boo!" The whoosh response happens very, very quickly.

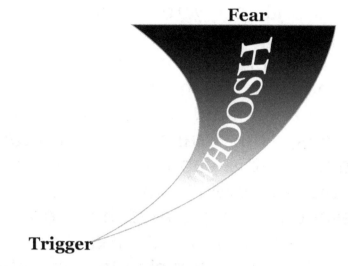

Figure 1: A whoosh of fear results from the trigger.

The Amygdala Learns to be Fearful

The amygdala learns to be fearful very easily, since its purpose is to protect you. When you were born, there were relatively few triggers that set off the alarm—loud noises and loss of support are two of the inborn fear triggers. Babies do not yet fear hot stoves, but the adult amygdala has learned to. As you mature, your amygdala learns to set off this alarm in response to a huge variety of triggers. You learn to be fearful of real dangers and to try to avoid them. This is the natural, normal, protective mechanism present in everyone.

In addition, for many people, certain animals, locations, voice tones, social situations, and means of transportation can develop the capacity to also set off this alarm, even though they may represent no objective danger on their own. Even emotional reactions like feeling trapped, anticipating rejection, or having doubts can set off alarms. In other words, your amygdala will set off a whoosh of fear in response to triggers that constitute no real danger. Psychologists call this conditioned learning. In this manner, fear responses can become habits of the brain.

People with unwanted intrusive thoughts have an amygdala that has learned to become afraid (i.e., clang the danger-warning bell) of certain *thoughts.* You were not born with a fear of these thoughts, and there is no *objective* reason to be afraid of them, but your amygdala has been conditioned to react when they appear in your mind. And, in our complicated world, there are a host of situations that aren't objectively dangerous, but can seem or feel dangerous. If your amygdala sets off the alarm in response to a harmless thought, you get a *false* alarm of danger: the bell clangs, you get an instant whoosh of fear, and it is very easy to think that there is *real* danger. The result is that thoughts *feel* dangerous, you try to fight them, and—of course!—they become stuck.

First Fear: The Amygdala's Automatic Alarm

The whoosh of fear triggered by your amygdala is sometimes called *first fear,* a term introduced by Claire Weekes (1969) in the 1950s. She described *first fear* as automatic. We might now say that triggering the alarm—first fear—is the default setting on your amygdala. We know that first fear is a response of your brain that is not under your conscious control. It is unstoppable.

But remember that the amygdala sends out many, many false alarms. Most first fears are actually false alarms. Only a very small percentage of them are indications of true danger. Your alarm system responds whenever it detects even the slightest hint of danger. A stuck thought—just like a "Boo!"—triggers this alarm because it was conditioned to do so.

Figure 2 shows a diagram of what goes on in your brain when someone yells, "Boo!" The Trigger is "Boo!" and the sound goes from your ear to a *switchboard* in your brain that is called the thalamus, which then very rapidly scoots it over to the amygdala. Your amygdala fires, and you have first fear. All of this occurs in the imperceptible time of about one-fifth of a second—the blink of an eye.

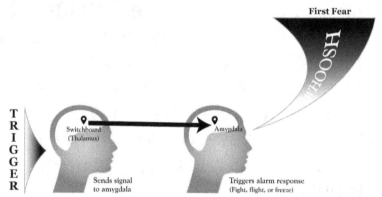

Figure 2: The thalamus sends the trigger signal to the amygdala, which fires and creates first fear.

So what makes first fear unstoppable and automatic? It actually has to do with how our brain is wired. Let's look more closely.

Two Paths to the Amygdala

In the 1990s, neuroscientists, including Joseph LeDoux (1998), made remarkable discoveries about how fear works in the brain. They discovered that brains are wired so that the amygdala receives signals from two distinct and separate pathways. Whenever your senses notice a *possible* danger—suppose it's a loud noise—your amygdala gets two signals about that possible danger. The "switchboard" (called the thalamus) in your brain sends out the signal in two directions at exactly the same time. One route is direct and extremely rapid, the route in figure 2. The other path makes its way through the cortex, or thinking part of your brain, and only then does it get to your amygdala. This longer path through the cortex takes about half of a second longer than the direct path.

So it reaches the amygdala about half of a second after the first signal.

If we were to diagram the route from the brain's "switchboard" (thalamus) to the amygdala, it would look something like figure 3.

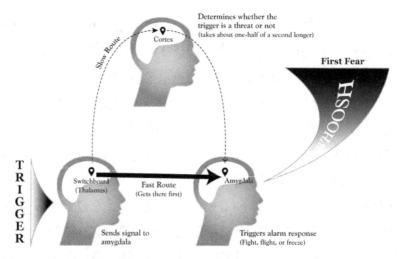

Figure 3: There are two separate paths to the amygdala.

Figure 3 shows the two paths. There is a fast route to the amygdala that bypasses the cortex, or thinking part, of your brain. The second, slower path goes through the cortex, which allows you to think about, or process, the meaning of the signal. The fast route is fast and fuzzy; the longer route is more precise. But you pay for that precision with some time. The longer route reaches the amygdala about half of a second *after* the fast route. So the messenger with a notice that something *might be* amiss gets there first, while the facts arrive afterward.

Let's return to the experience in which you are startled by your friend jumping out and yelling "Boo!" You jump, experience a whoosh of fright, and then calm down.

The sudden sound of "Boo!" was transmitted to your amygdala via the *fast route* that was first shown in figure 2. That set off your alarm response. As we mentioned, this fast route *bypassed your thinking brain* and got there very quickly. In fact, the arousal of the alarm response is the most rapid response in the human body! So when your friend yelled "Boo!" your reaction was immediate. This is an example of *first fear.*

Figure 3 shows first fear, but it also gives you an idea of what is happening with the second part of the signal—the part that is going to your thinking brain, your cortex. Figure 4 shows a diagram of this reaction that is occurring approximately one-fifth of a second after hearing the "Boo!

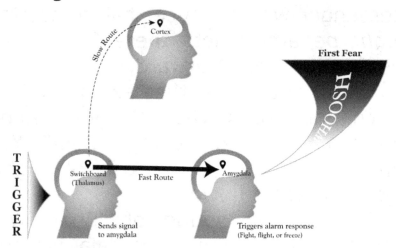

Figure 4: The whoosh of fear occurs before thinking can happen.

Notice that the signal has already made its way to the amygdala via the fast route and first fear has been triggered. Notice also that the other signal—traveling along the slower route and going first to the thinking part of your brain—*has not yet reached the amygdala.* Your amygdala is triggered before it gets the message from your cortex. In practical terms, the "Boo!" gives you a whoosh of fear *before you are able to think about it.* You get frightened before you know why. Your reaction is rapid, automatic, and unstoppable.

About a half second later, your amygdala gets the message from your thinking brain, or cortex. It tells you that the sound is just someone yelling "Boo!" and there is no danger involved. (After all, it might have been a gunshot.) It gives the message to your amygdala that it need not keep sounding the alarm, and you start to calm down. Within a few minutes, it is like it never happened.

Figure 5 illustrates the reduction of fear that occurs once the amygdala has received a signal from the cortex which says, in effect, "All clear. There is no need for alarm. This is just a harmless Boo! and you can stop clanging the alarm bell now."

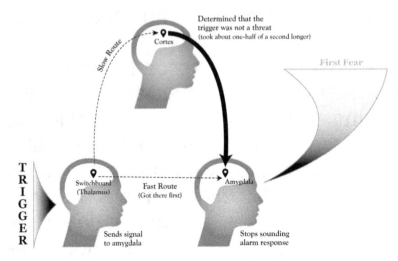

Figure 5: The cortex determines that there is no threat, and the amygdala stops sounding the alarm. First fear fades.

Notice in figure 5 that the whoosh of fear is quickly stopping, and first fear is fading away as the amygdala receives the message from the cortex that the trigger was not a threat.

We want to emphasize two points here. Number one is that first fear is unstoppable because it comes about before your conscious will has a chance to intervene. Willpower has nothing to with it because it is triggered before willpower has a chance to intervene. The second point is that first fear goes away quickly when you realize you are in no danger.

The Amygdala and Unwanted Intrusive Thoughts

But sometimes first fear doesn't go away quickly. In fact, sometimes first fear is just the fuse that sets off a whole series of fearful reactions. When that happens, this *second fear* sets the stage for unwanted intrusive thoughts to occur.

Let's imagine a situation very different from being startled by a friend. Let's suppose that your thinking brain (your cortex), instead of telling your amygdala that all is clear, tells your amygdala that there is, in fact, something to be frightened about. In that case, your amygdala would trigger the alarm again and would continue to sound the alarm for as long as your cortex warned of danger.

Specifically, let's say that you react with a whoosh of first fear to the intrusive thought, *I could jump off this balcony.* Then you may think, *What if I actually do it?* or *How can I be certain that I won't?* or *Does this mean I am suicidal without realizing it?* or even *Whatever is wrong with me must be serious.* These are the inner voices that keep the fear going. Your amygdala, stirred up by the voices, continues to sound the alarm, and you continue to be frightened.

How Inner Voices Create Unwanted Intrusive Thoughts

Our inner dialogue between Worried Voice and False Comfort creates a fear-increasing cycle by adding second fear to intrusive thoughts. A fear-decreasing cycle happens when this dialogue gives way to the voice of Wise Mind.

Fear-Increasing Cycle

Let's look more closely at how your inner voices work in the brain. First, remember that all three voices (Worried Voice, False Comfort, and Wise Mind) reside in the thinking part of your brain—the cortex. None of your voices have any role in the creation of the first whoosh of fear—what we call *first fear.*

However, all three characters feel the whoosh of first fear. True to form, Worried Voice is always duped. It believes immediately that where there is whoosh, there is danger. It does not cross Worried Voice's mind that most alarms are false alarms and that there are comparatively few real emergencies in life. Worried Voice automatically takes every alarm seriously whether it sounded in response to a creak in the attic, a skip of the heartbeat, or an intrusive thought.

Every time Worried Voice thinks of something else that could be amiss, the amygdala sends out another alarm. And, as long as Worried Voice asks the "What if (fill in something awful) is happening?" question, your amygdala continues to produce whooshes of fear.

As soon as this happens, False Comfort steps forward to try to silence Worried Voice. False Comfort tries by minimizing, pretending, explaining away, calming, and making a plan "just in case." But this only confirms for Worried Voice that the alarm was legitimate and needs to be dealt with. As we pointed out earlier, when False Comfort engages Worried Voice, then Worried Voice raises what-ifs once again. There is no getting away from it. False Comfort is not helping. You have now become stuck in an ongoing state of fright.

This is second fear—and as you try to fight the thought, you set the stage for an unwanted intrusive thought to take root.

Figure 6 represents the fear-increasing cycle that is going on with Worried Voice and False Comfort in your cortex.

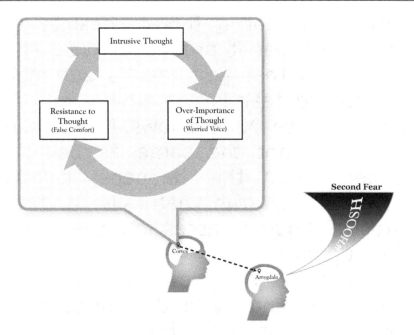

Figure 6: Worried Voice and False Comfort together create the fear-increasing cycle.

Fear-Diminishing Cycle

The best way to avoid second fear is to end the fear-increasing cycle by allowing Wise Mind to take over. It is only Wise Mind who realizes that the amygdala is just doing its job, that the thought is actually only a thought, and that the alarm is likely a false positive, needing only time to pass until it stops.

In your brain, Wise Mind is the voice from your cortex saying that your original thought, *What if I jump off this balcony?* is not a threat, despite the whoosh of fear it produced. Wise Mind remembers that first fear is automatic and second fear is something you can change. Wise Mind knows that feeling anxious is not the same as being in danger. When this happens, calming occurs on its own, naturally, and the intrusive thought passes into the stream of thoughts.

Figure 7 represents the fear-diminishing cycle that goes on in the cortex of your brain when you discover your Wise Mind and allow it to interact with Worried Voice.

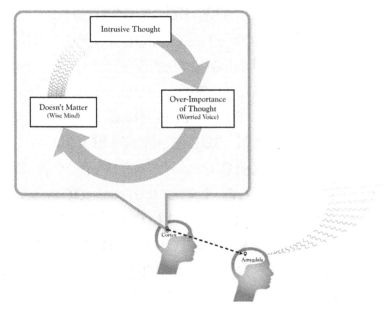

Figure 7: Wise Mind helps by not reacting to Worried Voice. This starts the fear-diminishing cycle.

Helpful Fact: Your Wise Mind knows that feeling anxious is not the same as being in danger.

Anxious Thinking

Your amygdala sets off the alarm response. You are ready to cope with threats. If the threat is real (a wild animal running toward you, an out-of-control car heading in your direction), the alarm response works exactly as it should, arousing the muscles, heart, and breath, enabling extra physical prowess needed to protect yourself (have you ever heard the stories of terrified mothers managing almost super-human strength to save their babies?). Your body and your brain are on emergency power.

However, emergency mode can also be turned on by anything that triggers a whoosh of fear. Things like social rejection, worries about health or finances, or the mere hint of disapproval from a boss can become conditioned triggers that set off the alarm response.

In cases like these—where the trigger is not a real danger, but rather an unsettling reminder of past unwanted thoughts, an ambiguous expression on someone's face that could possibly indicate rejection, or the thought of hurting a baby you love—this emergency mode is the opposite of helpful. In fact, it makes you wonder whether your mind is working properly. This state of mind is called *anxious thinking.* Anxious thinking comes directly from the hyper-alert state of the brain. It is part of the biology of arousal.

The world seems different when your amygdala has triggered the alarm response. When these changes occur and you are in the anxious thinking state, you are extremely vulnerable to unwanted intrusive thoughts. This alteration of awareness is part and parcel of the continuing alarm response. Here are some of the most important differences you will notice during anxious thinking.

Thought-Action Fusion

Ordinarily, the differences between thoughts and actions are clear. Anxious thinking creates an altered state of consciousness where scary thoughts can feel as frightening as scary behaviors. It is as if thoughts and actions feel fused together. Even though thoughts are triggering fears, people feel as if they are living through—not just thinking about—a dangerous experience. Thought-action fusion makes it seem that there is little difference between thinking about something and it actually happening. Thoughts no longer feel like a safe way to rehearse actions without consequences. What-ifs are not experienced as guesses or imaginings, they feel like visions of the actual future. Thoughts actually feel predictive. In addition, thought-action fusion makes it seem that thinking something is somehow morally equivalent to doing it—and therefore means something important about the thinker, so bad thoughts reveal a bad person.

All Risks Seem Unreasonable

When your amygdala is not triggering the alarm response, you understand that nothing in life is risk-free. Your actions in life are filled with what feels like reasonable risks. In contrast, your anxious thinking cannot accept any risks because thinking about something gives it a high probability of happening. What-if catastrophic thoughts seem likely to occur. Any thought that triggers the alarm makes ordinary risks feel unreasonable. Anxious thinking requires an absolute guarantee that a disastrous experience you might think about won't occur. You feel driven to ask for reassurances of safety, and you try to avoid the situations that trigger the feeling. And, of course, anxious thinking can't get that guarantee.

Thoughts Feel Sticky

Anxious thinking makes your scary thoughts hard to avoid. They seem stuck in your mind. No matter how much you tell yourself to think of something else, catastrophic thoughts come right back to intrude into your consciousness. Distractions are only partially helpful in getting your mind onto another subject, and they sometimes are no help at all. This is the neurological basis for the ironic process of the mind, which was first introduced in chapter 1. Effort used to *not* think of a thought actually makes it more intrusive.

Intolerance of Uncertainty

Life has plenty of uncertainties, and no one can predict the future. Most of the time, you are able to accept that nothing in life is risk-free and go on with your activities with little worry. But anxious thinking makes any uncertainty feel threatening. In addition, anxious thinking makes thoughts *feel* threatening. Certain thoughts are experienced as dangerous. It is very hard to hold onto the truism that thoughts and feelings are not facts.

Helpful Fact: Neither thoughts nor feelings are facts.

These are just a few of the ways that anxious thinking makes you vulnerable to unwanted intrusions. Your brain makes you sensitized and reactive to certain thoughts by altering the way your thoughts feel, and this begins the process. Now that you know how unwanted intrusive thoughts are created, the next chapter explains why you feel so frustrated. We are going to explain why nothing you have tried (up to now) seems to work.

CHAPTER 6

Why Nothing Has Worked

You have probably spent a lot of effort trying to get rid of your intrusive thoughts, usually without much success. It is likely that some time has passed since your first unwanted intrusive thought, and you have been struggling hard in frustrating attempts at controlling them, avoiding them, crowding them out, and otherwise trying to banish them from your mind. Perhaps you have tried other self-help techniques, sought advice from friends, or have even tried counseling or therapy. You may have told your therapist about your thoughts, or perhaps you have been too scared of what they might mean or what the therapist might do if he or she knew.

Three Factors That Get in the Way

There are three factors that explain why your efforts have not worked: sticky mind, paradoxical effort, and entanglement. We address each in this chapter. We review the effect of sticky mind, a biologically based tendency you were probably born with and need to understand. Next, we talk about paradoxical effort, a central concept introduced in previous sections. And finally, we introduce the idea of entanglement, which is essentially getting involved with the thought as if it were important. We will then give you real-life examples so you can identify where and how these three elements work to make your best efforts unsuccessful.

Sticky Mind

You may recall having different unwanted intrusive thoughts at different times in your life. They occur when your mind has become particularly "sticky," and you start paying way too much attention to your thoughts. "Sticky" mind is a term we use to describe the experience of having thoughts that should normally fly just once through your mind, but instead keep coming back, or repeat. Each time they return, they draw undue and undeserved attention, and feel stuck.

Whether you like it or not, you have a sticky mind, and you need to learn the factors that affect it. Sticky mind has a biological basis. It comes from a sticky brain. There are two factors that lead to it. One is genetic—this tendency runs in families and is associated with various inheritable traits and conditions relating to brain circuits and biochemistry. Most people with a sticky mind can identify other members of their families who have it as well, whether they own up to it or not. The second factor is stress. Minds tend to get stickier when they are fatigued, overwhelmed by good or bad events, and dealing with illness, stressful situations, or conflicting emotions. Minds are stickier if you are hungover, and for many, even a small amount of drinking can increase stickiness. A mind is stickier as soon as you start worrying about stickiness or checking on it to see if it is sticky. Stickiness can feel uncomfortable, but it is not dangerous or meaningful. And the really great news is that no matter what the causes (genetic or stress) are, you can learn to change your brain to become less sticky.

Sticky mind goes along with feeling anxious. One obvious aspect of the altered state of awareness we call anxious thinking is that threatening thoughts become extremely sticky. It is as if you are expecting danger and looking for it, so thoughts that feel dangerous—such as unwanted intrusive thoughts—stay glued to your mind. It's like flypaper.

Sometimes the theme of the content remains the same; sometimes it is different. Stickiness is a bit like those amusement park machines called "the claw," in which the arm comes out, wanders around, drops, and randomly picks up whatever is sticking up in the big jumble of junk in the cage. Whatever it picks up is not even worth the quarter you put in the machine.

Paradoxical Effort

You have certainly noticed something very strange and frustrating about your unwanted thoughts: the harder you try to not think them, the louder and more insistent they become. Effort seems to work backward. We have previously described this as the ironic effect—what happens when we try to control what is in our mind—but the more general principle is called "paradoxical effort."

If sticky mind can be compared to flypaper in the mind, then paradoxical effort can be seen as the old Chinese finger trap. Most of us played with this as kids—a simple woven bamboo tube. You stick your fingers in the ends, and then when you try to pull them out, the harder you pull, the tighter the grip of the tube, and the more stuck you get. The secret is figuring out that you have to push in, not pull out, to release your fingers.

The same thing is true for all of us in many aspects of life. Here are some other examples of the paradoxical effort:

- Trying with every bit of effort to fall asleep whether or not you are naturally sleepy
- Trying not to listen to the TV program playing in the room, while working to finish an assignment
- Trying to be spontaneously witty when you are feeling crabby
- Working hard to relax when you are very anxious
- Trying to laugh at something that does not strike you as funny
- Trying to ignore something you have just noticed
- Trying not to notice a foul smell
- Getting worked up is less effective when you have difficulty learning a new skill, such as learning the backhand swing in tennis and your instructor keeps telling you to "relax" and take a few deep breaths

It does not work to try to force your body to relax, to feel a particular emotion, or to force your mind to *not* have specific thoughts. And yet that is what most of us try (at least at first) when we are offended or scared by an unwanted intrusive thought. And then, when effort works backward, we think we should redouble our efforts. This is like trying to climb out of a hole by digging with a shovel, stopping a car by pressing the accelerator, or extinguishing a fire by fanning the flames.

Paradoxical effort is illustrated by the adage "less is more." But let's be clear: there are many times that effort works well in our lives. In fact, most of us believe (and for good reason) that hard work increases the chances of success. Not that hard work *guarantees* success, but people who work harder are generally more successful and fulfill their goals, on average, more often than people who work less hard. While this is true, there are, however, many important times in everyone's lives where less is more. And putting *less* direct effort into accomplishing a goal actually makes success *more* likely! This is paradoxical effort at work.

You might have tried to help someone with a problem or intervened in a feud between two other friends. There are times when your efforts are totally misconstrued, and, not only are you unsuccessful in helping heal a feud or solve a problem, but you get blamed for making it worse! In fact, if you had sat back and done nothing, the situation might have resolved on its own. This is one type of experience where less is more.

Here is another example: when you have a cut on your hand, it will eventually heal itself. Skin cells grow in their own time and lace together, and the cut is healed. But if you are impatient and keep checking it and pulling the Band-Aid off, you will pull off the forming scab and interfere with recovery. Passivity is actually far more efficient than effort. Sometimes you just have to figure out how to let time pass.

Yet another illustration: What's the best way to handle quicksand? The more you struggle to climb out, the more you sink. It is not immediately obvious, but the way to get out is to lie back and stop struggling! This increases your buoyancy, and you naturally float to the top where you are safe.

There are other areas where effort directly interferes with your goals. Learning is one of these activities.

Maximum learning requires an open, passive, curious attitude of attention. Judging yourself harshly while you are learning is not only unpleasant, it works against you. Have you had the experience of feeling pressure to learn something (a basketball play, French vocabulary, the plot of Hamlet, an app on your phone), and you keep getting it wrong? This is because you are putting pressure on yourself to learn, and this pressure interferes with the open, passive, attentive attitude that is best for learning. Once again, paradoxical effort means *less is more* in these circumstances.

Helpful Fact: Less is more when coping with unwanted intrusive thoughts.

Entanglement

Entanglement with a thought means that you have created an inner dialogue about the aggressive, sexual, nonsensical, or otherwise bewildering content running through your mind. You are judging it, arguing with it, or trying to reassure yourself about it. Or, you are trying to figure out some way to become less annoyed or less irritated by the intrusive nature of certain sounds, bodily feelings, or other intrusions. You become focused on the thought or sensation and your attempts to rationalize it, explain and understand its meaning, or just put it out of your mind. Entanglement can happen in a variety of ways, but most often, answering back or arguing with an intrusion is what keeps it going. Getting involved and entangled with unwanted intrusive thoughts makes them stronger and more insistent.

Here is one way to understand why: Imagine that you are walking down the street, on your way to your car, and a complete stranger walks by you and utters a disgusting comment, and then keeps on walking. You could decide to engage him by saying something back (perhaps: "How dare you!" or "That's disgusting"), but then he would have your attention, and he might say something else or even get aggressive. Most of you would agree that the best bet is to keep on walking. Don't even let him know that you heard him. Act as if you couldn't care less. Of course you know it occurred, and your feelings are also undeniable, but the best way to minimize the event is to not get involved.

Why would you act that way? *Not because you agree or think it is true.* But because you know it reduces the likelihood the person will continue his harangue. So you may very well feel frightened, but you will try to act as if you are ignoring the comment. Imagine that the person making the disgusting comment is an intrusive thought. Push back, and you are increasing the chances of another comment.

Entanglement with a thought often means that you are hijacked by your thought's aggressive, sexual, disgusting, frightening, or bewildering content. Getting involved and entangled with unwanted intrusive thoughts makes them stronger and more insistent.

We become entangled with thoughts when we take their message at face value. If we can see their message as junk, then it is much easier to ignore the content of the thought and focus instead on the meaning *behind* the content. If this seems difficult, then let's start with an example that we all know very well, which is from Dave Carbonell (2016), who has authored several self-help books on panic and worry (and hosts the popular website AnxietyCoach .com).

Imagine that you open the following e-mail addressed to you:

Congratulations! This is your lucky day. Your third cousin twice removed, who was the head of the [insert foreign country] Diamond Industry, has died and left $14 billion dollars to you. In order to collect this inheritance, please click on this link and provide us with your bank routing number. We will immediately transfer into your account the sum of $14 billion dollars. Again, accept our sincere congratulations.

Would you start excitedly imagining what it would be like to buy your own yacht, own your own private jet, or buy your own island? (We hope not, of course.) Because the words in this communication are not to be believed. The content is immaterial. This is a scam, and not an inheritance notice.

When you push the "send to spam" button, you have already disentangled yourself from the *content* of the e-mail. You have no problem buying the idea that the words should not be believed, and the e-mail is communicating a very different message: "Send me your money, sucker!"

So why is it so difficult to do the same thing with your unwanted intrusive thoughts? One reason is because your thoughts trigger your alarm response, and so the thoughts *feel* like they are correct. But come back to the realization that feelings aren't facts, and remember that anxiety is bluffing you once again.

Thoughts are not facts either. Thoughts are imaginations inside your mind. You could almost say that thoughts are a form of pretending. You forget about this as soon as you become more entangled with your thoughts. When emotional impact is added to a neutral thought, it becomes much easier to become entangled with it.

Helpful Fact: Neither thoughts nor feelings are facts.

Here is a demonstration of how entanglement can be increased. Try it out.

1. Write down the words "skill" and "grape." On a scale of 1 to 10, what emotional impact do each of these words have?

2. Remove the first letter from each word to get the words "kill" and "rape." Now what emotional impact do these words have?

3. Now write down the two original words once again: "skill" and "grape." Has the emotional impact changed?

You will likely find that the two original words now have more emotional impact than before. You have become entangled with these words because of the emotional connections to words you now can't help noticing. The words may no longer feel like "just words"—they feel dangerous or ominous or like something "bad." They may also feel unwelcome.

The basic message is that words are just words. They don't feel like anything unless you add an interpretation and a feeling—and then it is so easy to get entangled. Your internal dialogue can get kicked off in an instant. Entanglement increases as you become more involved with your internal dialogue. Responding to Worried Voice by trying to help keeps it going. False Comfort is the agent that increases entanglement.

Worried Voice: What if this doesn't work? What if I get so freaked out that I actually do what I'm afraid of?

False Comfort: Don't be silly, wipe that thought out of your...

Wise Mind: False Comfort, please don't respond to Worried Voice. Nothing good comes of it.

Worried Voice: OMG! Are you really going to subject me to these thoughts! I might just freak out.

Wise Mind: Not worth an answer.

Worried Voice: Did you hear what I said? I might actually do it!

Wise Mind: This is an intrusive thought. A thought is a thought.

Worried Voice: This is dangerous! I might have a nervous breakdown!

Wise Mind: I accept and allow thoughts.

Worried Voice: WHAT IF I CAN'T CONTROL MYSELF?

Wise Mind: I know there might be another intrusive thought that follows.

Worried Voice: I don't think I can stand this much longer!

Wise Mind: I'm letting time pass.

Worried Voice: I'm just so nervous about this. What if I never calm down?

Wise Mind: I'm floating and observing.

Worried Voice: What if I actually do it?

Wise Mind: No answer is needed.

Worried Voice: I'm not sure I can control myself.

Wise Mind: I'm allowing the thoughts.

Worried Voice: This is going on for such a long time. What if it never stops? (softly)

Wise Mind: I'm accepting the thoughts.

Worried Voice: I'm not sure I can control myself. (barely audible)

Wise Mind: Notice how soft Worried Voice becomes when no one responds.

Helpful Fact: Entanglement is a major factor in keeping intrusive thoughts going.

Ineffective Strategies

We will address the common but ineffective "coping strategies" of reassurance (both self-reassurance and reassurance from others), rational argument, prayer, "healthy living," and other counterproductive techniques designed to exert control and get rid of unwanted intrusive thoughts. Unfortunately, these popular suggestions for coping often encourage entanglement and paradoxical effort, and they fail to address sticky mind. So when you follow popular advice and don't get any relief, you might feel doomed and beyond help. Our message is that you are following approaches that *can't* work—not because you are doomed to misery—but because these approaches are simply the wrong way to tame your unwanted intrusive thoughts.

Reassurance is usually the first way people try to get rid of unwanted intrusive thoughts. Most people try to reassure themselves internally, by seeking reassurance from their own inner voices, from websites, and books, and then when that does not help, they seek reassurance from others. Reassurance involves entanglement by encouraging you to argue with the thoughts, as if they were valuable or meaningful or worthy of attention. And usually reassurance ends up with escalating efforts because it only works temporarily, and your mind comes back for more and better arguments, producing paradoxical effort. Prayer can inadvertently function as paradoxical effort if the source and meaning of the unwanted thoughts is misunderstood or spiritual doubts intrude when the thoughts do not go away. "Healthy living" can reduce general stickiness of the mind, but does nothing at all for entanglement. And "healthy living" can become a relentless preoccupation in a paradoxical effort to overcome and banish meaningless thoughts, leading to a rigid lifestyle, unnecessary deprivations, and more worries.

Self-Reassurance

Reassurance is one of the most common ways of pushing back. It is actually a way of talking back to your unwanted intrusive thought. At first, reassurance seems to help. Your anxiety goes down a bit, and you feel better. But then the doubts come back. You ask yourself how you can be *really* sure that these intrusive thoughts do not mean you are losing control. You wonder whether you have unconscious desires that might get the better of you if you aren't vigilant. Your thoughts come back in the form of *Yes, but what if?*—and then you have to find some other reassurance to the new what if question. So eventually the reassurance fails. Let's listen to a typical exchange between Worried Voice and False Comfort. Try as it may, Worried Voice never gets the certainty it seeks, and False Comfort gets progressively more frustrated.

Worried Voice: Tell me again that you believe I am a gentle person who would never knowingly harm anyone.

False Comfort: Of course, I keep telling you that I know you would never hurt a fly. You are the kindest and gentlest person I know.

Worried Voice: Okay, but there could always be a first time, you know. There must be some reason I'm having these thoughts. I read all the time about people who just *snap* and commit mayhem, and their neighbors always say they are shocked. They say, "He seemed like such a nice guy."

False Comfort: Yes. I know; I read about that also. But that is so rare, and you are not even angry at anyone.

Worried Voice: Maybe I don't realize how angry I am, and I could snap. You can't prove to me that I couldn't.

False Comfort: Well maybe I can't prove it, but I know in my heart you would never do it.

Worried Voice: Maybe you are just too nice to imagine such a thing.

False Comfort: No, I really believe in you.

Worried Voice: I don't just need you to believe in me; I need proof. You can't give me that, can you?

False Comfort: Well, maybe we should see a doctor to get some reassurance that you are not going to snap and do something horrible. Would you believe a doctor?

Worried Voice: See, I told you! You do think I need a doctor!

Reassurance from Others

You have probably asked at least one close person whether she or he thinks you will act on any of your unwanted intrusive thoughts. Perhaps a family member has noticed that you are acting differently, maybe avoiding a situation that you find triggering.

Here is just one example: You might be upset by the intrusive thought that you will blurt out blasphemous and vulgar words during church. Prior to this, you enjoyed going to church, both for the spiritual comfort and the social interaction. But your fear of acting on your thoughts leads you to avoid services, go to church late, or sit in the back of the congregation. Your family might notice this and ask you why you are staying away from something that seems to give you so much pleasure.

So you confess your thoughts and fears, and ask if they think you could possibly do such a horrible thing. If your family seems bewildered or frightened, you will take that reaction as still another piece of evidence that you might really lose control. If they say, "No, of course not. That is not like you, and I'm sure you would never do anything like that," you might feel temporarily relieved. But then, perhaps slowly at first, but inevitably, you will begin to doubt the comforting words. You soon start to argue with yourself.

Worried Voice: Jane says I would never do that, but how can she know for sure?

False Comfort: Jane is your friend and would never lie to you.

Worried Voice: Who's talking about lying? There are plenty of things Jane doesn't know about me. She might not realize how much these thoughts take over my mind. I have to work so hard to keep myself from losing control.

False Comfort: I think she knows you very well, and she sees what a good and spiritual person you are.

Worried Voice: That's what she can see. But I can see inside myself, and I can see my turmoil and impulses to sin.

False Comfort: So maybe you should tell the priest about this. Maybe God can grant you forgiveness.

Worried Voice: So even you believe I'm a bad person who needs forgiveness in God's eyes!

It's fine to ask others for reassurance once in a while, and just about everyone does that. But if you make it a habit whenever doubts arise, the additional reassurance continues the ongoing cycle. Some people actually become reassurance junkies and experience a constant need to get comfort and reassurance from family, friends, and the Internet. Some typical interactions with others around trying to get reassurance are discussed in chapter 7.

Prayer

The idea the prayers can work backward is a particularly bewildering and distressing realization if you take stock in a loving, forgiving God. Prayer is usually one of the first ways to cope with upsetting feelings and happenings. And, at first, there is often a welcome sense of relief that your thoughts will be removed by God and that God's good presence will look after you. You feel safer when you are connected to God.

However, the feeling of relief and reassurance—even if it comes from the belief in a loving God—is still a way of pushing back against the thought. By asking for the thought to be removed, you are taking the thought seriously and thereby giving it more power than it deserves. This leads to additional entanglement, which always functions to increase the frequency and distress associated with these thoughts. So the prayer feels ineffectual, and there is a tendency to pray harder, to doubt that God is listening, or to think you are somehow beyond God's forgiveness.

Some people experience a crisis of faith when this strategy fails. But this is simply because this kind of supplication prayer continues the push-back effort and results in even more entanglement. It does not mean that you are forsaken. It is just how the mind works.

Unwanted intrusive thoughts always feel that they are *not you.* Not that they are coming from outside of yourself, but rather that for some inexplicable reason, these thoughts pop up and keep running through your mind. Psychologists call these types of feelings *ego alien* or *ego dystonic.* To some degree, this is how they feel to everyone who has them.

Let's be clear here: It does *not* feel like someone is out to get you or that you are hearing voices from aliens. It is different from paranoia. Rather, it feels more like your thoughts reflect actions or feelings that seem so alien. Some people of faith wonder if they are temptations of Satan or voices of perverse spirits. Most religions have some way to describe these particular experiences that do not seem part of the normal flow of the mind. The content of your thought feels so unlike you—of the sort, *Oh my God, would I really do such a horrible thing to an innocent child?* that some people think that it must be some evil force taking over them. If this happens to you, you might then begin to worry that you are outside of God's grace and feel even more upset that your prayer appears to be unanswered.

Helpful Fact: Unwanted intrusive thoughts feel like they are *not* you.

For this reason, ritualized prayer as a way of coping with unwanted intrusive thoughts tends to be counterproductive and is not recommended as a helpful approach.

But please don't take this as a suggestion that you should abandon your religious beliefs or your prayers. If you believe in a loving, providential God—or even if you just consider yourself a spiritual person—then by all means you are encouraged to stay with your usual prayers and worship. However, to ask for God's forgiveness or to remind yourself that, for example,

"God is good and loving and will take care of me" *each time* you have an intrusive thought (and hoping it will take the thought away) is actually engaging the thought, adding to entanglement and—despite some temporary relief—leading to further intrusive thoughts.

When you do pray, ask God to help you to understand and believe in this book you have been led to, rather than ask for the thoughts to be taken away. He knows you have been struggling to be good. He wants you to take the leap of faith this book is advocating. Your thoughts are not a punishment, but they are indeed a challenge.

Healthy Living

A lot of people think that unwanted intrusive thoughts and other signs of anxiety or emotional distress come from stress, so they try to reduce stress in order to feel better. It's common to double down on healthy behavior whenever we are feeling overwhelmed or out of control. We define healthy behavior as eating right, getting a reasonable amount of exercise, cutting down on alcohol and any other drugs, finding a sleep routine that works, and avoiding obvious forms of stress. Changing a job, breaking up an unhealthy relationship, and taking a vacation may reduce stress, but they will not lead to a lasting solution to the problem of unwanted intrusive thoughts.

There are plenty of good reasons to eat right and get good exercise. In fact, it is clear that healthy eating and healthy exercise improve your mood and lower anxiety. But unfortunately, these activities alone won't stop your unwanted intrusive thoughts.

There is a relationship between stress and fatigue, on the one hand and unwanted intrusive thoughts on the other. Eating, exercising, and sleeping well, as well as avoiding drugs and reducing stress, may reduce the intensity and frequency of intrusions. Conversely, poor eating and sleeping, lack of exercise, drinking alcohol, and a highly stressful lifestyle tends to increase the intensity and frequency of unwanted intrusive thoughts. But—and here is the point we would like you to take away—healthy living will not *cure* unwanted intrusive thoughts, and unhealthy living will not *cause* them. While healthy living may temporarily reduce your sticky mind, it has no effect at all on the two other factors—paradoxical effort and entanglement—that function to keep your intrusive thoughts going.

Other Counter-Productive Techniques

Techniques for ridding yourself, bypassing, or avoiding unwanted intrusive thoughts are attempts at *control.* The problem is that attempts to control are prime examples of paradoxical effort and are guaranteed to increase entanglement. Trying to control the thoughts is entirely the wrong attitude. It ignores the fact that the thoughts are meaningless and harmless, and don't require controlling. The attempt to control them reinforces the wrong message. It is an example of paradoxical effort: it works backward. It suggests urgency, importance, and danger, when none exists.

You may be aware of the Serenity Prayer recited daily by people in twelve-step programs:

> God grant me the serenity to accept the things I cannot change; courage to change the things I can; and the wisdom to know the difference.

In this case, what cannot be changed is the arrival of the unwanted thought—it just happens—and the first fear or initial jolt of emotion is what arrives with it. Our consistent message is that what *can* be changed is your reaction to that experience. That is what you are trying to do.

It does take lots of courage to just let it happen and not react to the false alarms: you have to just let the thought be there and trust that it is okay to do that—even while you cannot be 100 percent absolutely certain.

And this is why techniques, if applied with the wrong attitude, can actually make your discomfort increase, rather than the opposite. Don't think of coping techniques as a form of nonchemical tranquilizers. Even if techniques enable you to *temporarily*

lower your distress, they will not solve
the problems of entanglement and
paradoxical effort.

Here is an illustration of how
technique application can either be
helpful or make things worse.
Abdominal, slow, or diaphragmatic
breathing that is undertaken with the
goal of making anxiety or thoughts go
away will not ultimately be helpful. In
contrast, breathing slowly and naturally
while you allow unwelcome thoughts to
be there can indeed be helpful. If
calming methods are applied without
the intention of banishing thoughts—but
simply to be okay while continuing to
experience the thoughts—there is no
need for the monitoring or checking to
see what has happened to the thoughts.

Popular Advice

Following is a list of techniques
recommended by popular magazines,
friends, family, and even therapists.
Well-intentioned people frequently
suggest that such coping techniques are
goals, and if you practice them
diligently, you can learn to manage your

anxiety. You will then have these tools at your fingertips and be able to use them successfully whenever the need arises. Unfortunately, they are all attempts to *control* your thoughts that end up backfiring. None of them, in fact, is ultimately helpful.

The problem is that they stop working even though they may seem helpful at first, as you no doubt have already discovered. There is a very good reason why they stop working, and it is not your fault. These techniques convey the wrong attitude and send the wrong message. *Coping* is not the goal here. Coping does not provide lasting recovery because it fails to address an essential change of attitude. Our goal is much more enduring and profound than mere coping. We want you to reach the point where you do not care whether the thoughts come or not. We would like you to turn off the alarm system in reaction to these thoughts so your amygdala no longer needs to warn of danger. We want you to change your relationship with the thoughts so they no longer cause distress. This reduces dread and stickiness so ultimately the thoughts will cease to bother you at all.

See if you can recognize one or more of these pieces of advice that you have tried and have not found helpful for very long.

1. Try to relax by exerting more willpower.

   The suggestion here is to put in more effort, but unfortunately, what you resist persists, and you inadvertently produce paradoxical effort. It is impossible to force yourself to relax by using willpower.

2. Stop worrying about it; you will make yourself sick.

   The implication here is that the worry is more dangerous than the thoughts. This is called meta-worry, and leads to more concerns, more anxiety, more stickiness, and more intrusive thoughts, not fewer.

3. Everything will be okay; trust me; I promise.

   Clearly this is the voice of False Comfort, sometimes called empty reassurance. Your own Worried Voice will respond almost immediately with "Yes, but..."

4.   Calculate the probability of that happening.

This is often called *rational disputation* or *reasoning.* Unfortunately, your fearful Worried Voice starts arguing because it does not matter how likely something might be; it only matters that it would be terrible if it actually happened. This increases entanglement through paradoxical effort.

5.   Don't think about it; think about something else.

Distraction is a direct invitation to the ironic process, an example of paradoxical effort we introduced in chapter 1. The effects of distraction are momentary, and you can become desperate, frustrated, disgusted, or fearful when the thoughts insist on returning.

6.   Think happy thoughts or affirmations.

This is called *suppression* and has the same problem. The implication is that these thoughts are dangerous or that that they indicate bad things about you. This increases entanglement and makes the thoughts more sticky in the long run. It is the very opposite of the attitude of acceptance.

7. Have more faith. Pray to have the thoughts removed.

As we discussed earlier in this chapter, this kind of prayer can backfire in demoralizing and devastating ways.

8. Stay positive; negative attracts negative.

This is called *magical thinking* by psychologists and is an example of entanglement with thoughts. There is no evidence that thoughts affect actual facts in the world. They are thoughts. Try thinking yourself into a sudden death. Or, try using your thoughts to push over a bookcase. Nothing happens. And the effort to think only positive thoughts is a form of paradoxical effort that results in more negative ones.

9. Cut out sugar and caffeine, try this tea, and exercise it away.

As we discussed earlier, it is not true that unwanted intrusive thoughts are caused by stress and that lifestyle changes will take them away. They are stress-sensitive, but not due to stress. Reduction in stress can reduce some aspects of stickiness but has no effect on entanglement or paradoxical effort.

10.   Dump the boyfriend or the job, take a vacation, and don't watch the news.

This is a formula for avoidance, which is absolutely the most effective fuel for keeping unwanted intrusive thoughts fired up and active. It makes two mistakes. The first is the implication that unwanted intrusive thoughts are meaningful messages, even if they seem inconsistent with what you believe. This is an example of entanglement. So if your unwanted thoughts are negative statements about your beloved boyfriend, then this technique implies you should respect the message and get rid of him and you will have no peace until you do. Or if you are having intrusive doubts about your mental health and otherwise feel okay, it implies that you should treat yourself as if you were emotionally fragile and get rid of anything disturbing in your life. The second mistake is two-fold: first, the idea that having intrusive thoughts means you are falling apart and second, that a big life change or stress reduction will fix the problem. Avoidance solves nothing.

11. Snap this rubber band every time you think it.

This technique was once called thought-stopping and was actually recommended by therapists before a full understanding of unwanted intrusive thoughts was developed. It is a form of punishment and results in a sore wrist and increased frequency of thoughts. It gives the incorrect message that thoughts should be avoided, an attitude that increases both paradoxical effort and entanglement.

12. Practice meditation and yoga, and the thoughts will go away.

Meditation and yoga can both be helpful in reducing the tendency to have a sticky mind and to get entangled with thoughts, but if they are done with the intention of banishing or conquering thoughts instead of relating to them differently, they will not be helpful.

Techniques can be applied in active or fighting ways that produce desperation, frustration, and fear, and make the thoughts stickier, increase entanglement, and become prime examples of paradoxical effort. Or they can be applied in passive ways, which reinforce the fact that the thoughts do not constitute a danger, do not need to be fought, have no special significance, and will go away on their own once they are left alone.

The best perspective is one that is not at all obvious. Instead of battling with the problem, you can try to willingly and intentionally go toward uncertainty and distress. When you do not recoil from your own thoughts, they lose their power. When you face the dragon, he turns out to be made of fluff.

By now you should have quite an understanding of unwanted intrusive thoughts and why so many of your best-effort attempts to get rid of them have been unsuccessful. A comprehensive list of the varieties of intrusions has allowed you to identify your own kinds of thoughts, and you have learned how your brain works to automatically trigger your alarm response when it encounters sensitized thoughts, sensations, and memories. You have the information to bust the nine myths that contribute to stuck thoughts. And we have demonstrated how unwanted intrusive thoughts get stuck precisely because they are not you and feel inconsistent with your beliefs and values. You have come to understand that the worst part of every intrusive thought is not the thought itself, but your internal commentary that follows. Reducing the commentary will reduce your distress. We explained how the three factors of sticky mind, paradoxical effort, and entanglement all work to keep these unwanted intruders alive.

So now is the time to apply what you have learned and continue with your progress toward recovery. Your goal is nothing less than being done with these intruders and keeping them from making your life so miserable. The challenge is twofold: The first is to learn the proper attitude to adopt each time an unwanted intrusive thought pops in your mind. The second is to retrain your brain so your newly learned attitudes become your habitual, or default, reaction. Your goal is to allow these threatening thoughts to become less and less important so your relationship to the content of these thoughts changes profoundly. The aim is not just to manage the anxiety and distress each time it arises, but to actually overcome the apprehension that unwanted intrusive thoughts could ever torture you again. In the next chapter, you are going to create new circuitry in your brain that reacts in a fundamentally different way to these intrusions. Let's continue our work together to turn your disturbing unwanted intrusive thoughts into things of the past.

CHAPTER 7

How to Handle Thoughts When They Happen

This chapter is about developing a way to reduce your distress from unwanted intrusive thoughts, whether they are in response to a recent trigger or they just seem to pop up out of the blue. Your attitude toward these thoughts makes all the difference, and the attitude that works is called *acceptance.* This chapter defines what acceptance means—and what it doesn't mean—and provides specific steps for achieving it.

First, we present the six steps for best coping with each intrusive thought as it occurs. This provides a detailed outline to guide your own response to these intruders. Next, we present the three most common classes of reactions that get in the way of successfully following these guidelines. Then, we present a variety of illustrative stories, or metaphors, that demonstrate the therapeutic attitude of acceptance.

As we have discussed, the distress over intrusions and the struggle with them tends to make them stronger and stickier over time. Yet, under most circumstances, repeating things gets boring, and we get used to them and stop paying attention. So why don't you just get used to these kinds of thoughts? We have all been taught that if you face your fears, they will go away and that exposure is what helps. If you are afraid of elevators, get on them over and over again, and you will get over your fear of them. If you are afraid of public speaking, take a course in which you learn to do it every week. So why doesn't this work with unwanted thoughts? Surely you are getting plenty of exposure already.

The problem is that *exposure must be done the right way.* Otherwise, it can have the opposite effect and can actually empower and reinforce intrusions. Exposure that is done right must be willing and free of struggle. Many commonsense methods that seem to be helping you cope in the moment don't fit these conditions. Specifically, your struggle with intrusive thoughts is what keeps them coming back. As a result, despite your best efforts and intentions, you are actually prolonging the problem.

There is a difference between coping with each unwanted intrusive thought as it occurs and embarking on a program to be done with them. You are reading this book because intrusive thoughts are making your life (or the life of someone you care about greatly) quite miserable. So you want to know what to do *right now,* as each intrusive thought crams into your mind. That approach makes perfect sense, and in this chapter we present the most effective ways of coping with each unwanted intrusive thought *as it occurs.* People have found this enormously helpful because commonsense methods of coping—as discussed in previous chapters—most often just empower the next intrusive thought.

When you are simply trying to make the best of each intrusive thought, your goal is to get through that particular episode of intrusions with the least amount of pain and distress. Learning to better cope with the next one is secondary to the main goal of just getting through the experience. As a result, there is often little long-term change. You have already learned that your old methods of coping are not helpful in the long run because they usually involve trying to avoid, reassure, justify, or argue with the thoughts. And each one of these techniques empowers the thought and makes it more potent and scary the next time.

But here is some great news for you. Every bit of information you learned so far has worked to change your perspective and understanding of intrusions. Every myth about thoughts you uncovered has helped change the way you relate to these thoughts. And you now understand why commonsense methods to cope actually increase the problem.

This chapter has two goals. First, to provide a better way of coping each time you experience an intrusive thought and second, to retrain your brain. These two work together. As you are coping better, you are automatically beginning the process of retraining your brain to be less fearful.

Six Steps to Reduce Distress Over a Thought

There are six essential steps for coping with each unwanted intrusive thought. If you practice them regularly, you will be breaking bad habits and training your brain to be less susceptible to future intrusive thoughts. You can remember the six steps by committing the acronym RJAFTP to memory:

1.   **R:** recognize
2.   **J:** just thoughts
3.   **A:** accept and allow
4.   **F:** float and feel
5.   **T:** let time pass
6.   **P:** proceed.

You can make up a sentence to help you remember the steps (for example, Robert just ate fries, tacos, and pie).

Step 1: Recognize

Pause and label. Say to yourself something like, "Right now I am having a thought that intrudes into my awareness. This is an intrusive thought. It has caught my attention because of how it feels."

Worried Voice: What if I kill my son?

Wise Mind: This is an intrusive thought. You can tell because it feels so awful.

This is a process of observing yourself as you experience each intrusive thought. What emotions do you feel? What sensations make up the feeling that accompanies the intrusion? You are attempting to remain as mindful as possible, watching yourself from a curious and nonjudgmental viewpoint.

Both of these actions are counterintuitive since your alarm response is already labeling the thought as *dangerous* and pumping up your body to fight or flee the thought. So your goal is to be willing to allow these thoughts even when you are not expecting them and to try not to be blindsided by their appearance. That gives you the best chance of interrupting your ingrained response long enough to say to yourself, "Wait!

This is one of those thoughts that feel dangerous, but isn't. This is an intrusive thought."

There is another element that makes this even harder. You can never be 100 percent certain that you are correct. There is always the possibility that you might be wrong.

Remember that whenever you experience the effects of anxious thinking, having even a 99 percent probability of certainty still isn't enough. There is no risk that feels reasonable. You are looking for total and complete certainty. This fight for certainty fuels your Worried Voice and makes it harder for you to label your thought as an intrusive one. You focus on the content of your thought, rather than the result of a false alarm triggered by an eager amygdala. So the action of labeling helps you to practice the art of allowing reasonable uncertainty in your life. We will talk more about this important element when we discuss ways to practice in chapter 8.

Helpful Fact: Certainty is a feeling and not a fact.

Step 2: Just Thoughts

Remind yourself: dig up the information you already know—that these thoughts are automatic and you can *safely* leave them alone. Say lightly to yourself, "These thoughts are automatic and are best left alone."

Simply stating these facts gently to yourself helps to disentangle yourself from your thoughts.

Worried Voice: Oh, no!

Wise Mind: Thoughts are just thoughts. Junk thoughts are still junk thoughts. No need to do anything.

Reminding yourself helps you differentiate between what you can and cannot control. As we have shown, the thought and the resultant whoosh of distress is automatic, which is what we call the first fear. This lies outside of your control. But remember: you have the capacity either to increase that fear into second fear or to leave it alone. Leaving it alone allows your natural calming process to take over.

Leaving these thoughts alone is a way to avoid entanglement. Anything you do at this point that involves effort tends to push first fear into second fear. This is the point where paradoxical effort prolongs the thought and makes it seem more dangerous. Think of the Chinese finger trap, in which you have to do the opposite of your commonsense reaction to free yourself. Leaving the thought alone may feel like the opposite reaction, but it is the best way to release the grip on the thought. Think of having a tug of war with thoughts and what happens if you just drop the rope.

Your job is to remind yourself of what you already know. Intrusions, whooshes of fear, and the tendency to label the thought as dangerous all occur very quickly. But you are working to remember at that moment to call up your Wise Mind and say, "I can sit this one out."

Step 3: Accept and Allow

Accept and allow the thoughts in your mind. Do not try to push them away. This is a complicated suggestion, and many people ask questions about it and find it difficult to comprehend. We will talk about this later in more detail, but for the present, your job is *not* to distract, *not* to engage, and *not* to reason away.

Worried Voice: What if I kill him?

False Comfort: No, you won't. You are just tired. Maybe you are unconsciously angry at your son. Maybe you ate some bad meat. I just know there must be some explanation for your bad thought.

Wise Mind: Accept and allow means leave them alone. Let them do whatever they do. Just observe.

Don't allow yourself to start exploring the ideas or content of your thoughts. Don't try to come up with a plan or solve any problem that appears to be created by your thought. When you do this, you are trying to figure out the answer to a problem that has no answer. Furthermore, it is not a problem!

What does it mean to *accept* and *allow* the thoughts? Accept does not mean "I am stuck forever with these thoughts and the misery around them, so I just have to put up with them." It also does not mean "I have to accept the content of these thoughts that says I am bad, crazy, or flawed." A*ccept* and *allow* means that you are *actively* allowing the thoughts to be there, not wishing they were gone, because this attitude helps you grasp that the thoughts are unimportant. They do not require any attention or response. You might even welcome the thoughts as another opportunity to teach the brain a different way.

Accept and allow also recognizes that you might very well get another intrusive thought. So when you are actively allowing the thoughts to be there, you are also letting yourself know that another one might follow.

There is a saying that goes, "The devil is in the details." This refers to the truism that mistakes are usually made in the small details of a task. Sometimes apparently small details in your reaction can make the difference between allowing and engaging. There is a critical difference between thinking *This is an intrusive thought* or *Thoughts are just thoughts* as opposed to *This thought is not true.* The first two statements label the thought and disengage from its content. The second evaluates the content of the thought (Is it a true or false message?). It also adds a dash of self-reassurance about the content, thereby suggesting the content is worth considering. So the statement *This is an intrusive thought* allows the intrusive thought, while *This is not true* engages with it. The change of attitude from engaging to accepting and allowing can be very subtle.

Here is one way to understand what it means to accept, not push away, and also not engage with each intrusive thought: The voice of False Comfort always spurs on Worried Voice. Not engaging with each unwanted intrusive thought involves silencing False Comfort. That robs Worried Voice of the fuel it needs to keep spouting fears. Silencing False Comfort is one way of refusing to engage with your intrusive thought.

Remember that you can expect to feel the initial alarm. This is your amygdala doing its job. But right after that whoosh of distress arrives, *your* job is to keep False Comfort in check. Each of the following are habits of False Comfort, whom you are trying to silence. Stay away from them. When you notice False Comfort stepping forward, gently withdraw your attention and participation.

False Comfort wants you to

- engage the thoughts in any way possible
- answer any question the thought poses
- push the thoughts out of your mind
- figure out what your thoughts "mean"
- try to determine whether the thought is "true" or "false" (but remember it is a thought, not a fact)
- analyze why the thought pops up now
- convince yourself that you would never do what the thoughts are saying

- change your behavior so you avoid the possibility of acting on your thoughts
- offer reassurance one way or another.

Every time you silence False Comfort, you minimize the commentary that follows your intrusive thought. As you are learning, the major problem with unwanted intrusive thoughts is not so much the thought itself, but the internal dialogue that follows. If you notice Worried Voice and False Comfort struggling with each other, find your way to Wise Mind, who will tell you it is a conversation not worth the effort.

Accept and allow is actually more of an attitude than a technique. It is an attitude that acknowledges that what you resist tends to persist. It is an attitude of willingness. When you allow thoughts to be there, you are no longer struggling. The thoughts lose their power. You have the attitude of Wise Mind. As you practice handling your unwanted intrusive thoughts with this new attitude, you will find that your old habits are initially hard to break. You are not yet at the point where you fully believe the thoughts are unimportant, but that is your goal.

> **Helpful Fact:** Accept and allow is more of an attitude than a technique.

Step 4: Float and Feel

Float above the fray and allow the *feelings* to just stay there. Return to the present whenever you notice you are out front in an imagined future. Move from all that thinking into your current senses. (What can you see, hear, smell, and touch?) Concentrate on *what is* as opposed to *what if.* Surrender the struggle.

Worried Voice: I can't stand this. I am having these thoughts. I won't sleep tonight if I can't get rid of them.

False Comfort: Can't you push them away? You need to be relaxed and rested for the exam tomorrow. Just think about something else. A sleeping pill might get you to sleep.

Wise Mind: I'm watching you right now. You are entangled in your what-if thoughts. Imagining the future like this does not allow the present reality. Notice the floor under your feet or the sounds of the heating system. Focus on what you can sense right now. I'm sensing your frustration; feel it and let the thoughts just be where they are. Sensations change from moment to moment, so do thoughts.

Floating above the fray is a way to remove yourself from the turbulent experience. It is not about struggling with the thoughts. You will eventually observe your discomfort from a curious point of view, as opposed to immediately labeling it as dangerous or unendurable. Floating above the fray is connecting to your Wise Mind. Floating is an attitude of non-active, non-urgent, non-effortful observation. It is non-distressed, uninvolved, and passive. It is nonjudgmental. It is allowing thoughts to be there for as long as they happen to be. *It is the opposite of entanglement.*

Step 5: Let Time Pass

Allow time to pass. Don't urge it on. Observe your anxiety and distress from a curious, disinterested point of view. Do not keep checking to see if this is working; just let the thoughts be there. They are thoughts. There is no hurry.

Worried Voice: I don't know how much longer I can tolerate this. I'm freaking out; when will this be over?

False Comfort: Let me read the coping techniques again because they don't seem to be working. Let's do affirmations: I am good person; I am a good person; I am a good person. It says here that these bad thoughts usually pass in a few minutes; let's count down the time.

Wise Mind: As far as I'm concerned, I could sit with these thoughts all day. My discomfort has nothing to do with being in any danger. These are just thoughts.

Allowing time to pass is one of the most important skills for recovery.

Remember that any thought that produces a repeated feeling of urgency is a sign of anxiety. A feeling of urgency is discomfort, not danger. It comes automatically with the thoughts, but it is not a signal for action. Counting down until you feel better propels you into the future, increases your discomfort, and makes you fight the thought even harder. Checking to see if the steps are working is yet another way of stimulating them. Slow down. Let it be. You are dealing with discomfort, not danger. Time allows your normal calming reaction to take effect, on its own, naturally.

Helpful Fact: The feeling of urgency that comes with an unwanted intrusive thought is a false message from your brain.

While you are allowing time to pass, if you notice that you have reentered thoughts about the future and your usual catastrophic, worried, or judgmental commentaries, gently escort your mind back to the present. Notice that you are having some meaningless thoughts in the present. Whenever you notice that you are recoiling from the thoughts and struggling with them, go back to floating and letting time pass. There is no hurry. There is no danger. Pay attention to your feelings and sensations. Encourage your Wise Mind to stay present. Slow your pace. You can intentionally slow down, talk more slowly, and walk and act more slowly. You don't have to crowd out thoughts or feelings. You might very well discover new sensations, new thoughts passing through your mind, and perhaps even new memories. Notice them as they pass through your awareness.

Step 6: Proceed

Even while you are having the thoughts, *continue* whatever you were doing prior to the intrusive thought.
Worried Voice: I feel really shaky. What if it comes right back?

False Comfort: Rest for a while. That should help. Take some time off. You just dodged a bullet. Don't stress yourself too much. Take it easy.

Wise Mind: Feeling shaky is just distressing, not dangerous, and the thought that it might come back is just another thought. It does not matter if a meaningless thought comes back. I'm going on with my routine, my activities, and my life.

Remember that you are practicing new ways of relating to your thoughts. The most effective way to rob them of power is to continue doing the things you were doing and had intended to do prior to the thoughts. Imagine that unwanted intrusive thoughts are terrorists of the mind. Just as terrorists work by making people change the way they live, feeling compelled to abandon what you are doing is giving power to the message of terror. Even if you are feeling afraid (that's your amygdala doing what it is supposed to do) and even if your intrusions return, your most powerful response is to continue with your life as if nothing has happened.

You are in the process of learning a new way to deal with unwanted intrusions so there is no more empowering and reinforcing the next distressing thought. Your new attitude will rob it of its sting. Now let's look at some of the most common obstacles to this goal.

Enemies of Acceptance

There are three reactions that typically occur right after an episode of intrusive thoughts. All are common. They typically provoke entanglement and paradoxical effort and undermine the ability to practice the six steps above. Understanding how these typical reactions interfere with recovery makes it much easier to practice acceptance when an unwanted intrusive thought shows up. They are guilt, doubt, and urgency.

Guilt

Guilt (and the reassurance-seeking it often stimulates) gets in the way of adopting the attitude of acceptance. After having gone through an episode of unwanted intrusive thoughts, some people experience a wave of guilt. They then ask others for reassurance that they aren't a bad person or that no one was harmed by thinking such thoughts. We call this *externalizing the commentary.* It means that you are taking your internal interchange between your own Worried, False Comfort, and Wise Mind voices and playing that out with real people in your life. This is a form of reassurance-seeking: you are asking others to tell you that your thoughts are okay. And, like any reassurance, it provides temporary relief but ends up adding power to the intrusion.

Guilt can be associated with an enormous range of intrusive thoughts. Harming or self-harming intrusions can bring guilt in the form of *What kind of person am I that I would even have such a thought?* You can feel unholy or sinful after having blasphemous thoughts. When asking others for reassurance in situations like this, you also run the risk of piling on additional guilt for upsetting or frightening them. You also may seek reassurance that having those bad thoughts does not reflect on your character, which reinforces the voice of False Comfort.

Remember that your goal is to silence False Comfort.

Here is a typical internal commentary or dialogue, where someone with unwanted intrusive thoughts is debating with himself.

Worried Voice: Wise Mind keeps saying it is okay to think these thoughts, but I believe that "lusting in your heart" is just as bad as actually doing it.

False Comfort: Worried Voice, you don't even go to church; what is all this moralizing? I asked my priest, and he said everybody thinks bad thoughts; you should just ask for forgiveness, and you will be forgiven.

Wise Mind: Slow down. I see no need to ask for forgiveness. That applies only when you have actually willfully done something bad, a situation where you had a choice and chose poorly. We are not responsible for things that happen when there is no choice or control. It is simply not true that we can control what pops into our mind. We can control what we choose to do, but not the automatic thoughts that just show up.

And here is how seeking *external reassurance* goes. You can see how similar it is to the internal dialogue that just cranks up the volume of Worried Voice and is not helpful.

Self: I just had a terrible sexual thought about my niece. And she is so innocent and sweet.

Friend: You know you would never do anything. Everyone has bad thoughts.

Self: Not as bad as these.

Friend: You need to distract yourself. Just think of something else.

Self: I try, but I can't.

Friend: Ask God to take the thoughts away and forgive you.

Self: He is not listening to my prayers.

Friend: Of course He is.

Self: What if I am beyond redemption?

Here is a typical exchange that happens when someone has just had an unwanted intrusive thought.

Sam: I had these thoughts about the woman who works next to me. I feel terrible.

John: From time to time everyone has sexy thoughts about other people. Even Jimmy Carter "lusted in his heart." Forget about it, it's nothing.

Sam: But suppose I actually do something? My wife would be so hurt, and she'd probably divorce me.

John: Whoa! Buddy. You are just talking about sexy thoughts. Now you are imagining a divorce! You're fine. Just leave it alone. Or enjoy it. Don't worry about it.

Sam: So you think I shouldn't feel guilty?

John: You sure are making a big deal out of this. Maybe you should feel just a little guilty.

Sam: I feel terrible.

John: What's got into you? I thought we were going to watch the game.

Sam: Well, I just need to know I am not a bad person.

John: I already told you! Would you just stop this?

Here is another:
Kate: I think I may have postpartum depression. I keep having a really scary thought. Everyone does, right?

Janet: Lots of women have a hard time. You are not getting much sleep you know.

Kate: Yes, but I keep thinking I might hurt my baby. It is horrible.

Janet: You mean drop him accidentally? Or he might slip in the bathtub?

Kate: I am scared to say this out loud. But no, more like on purpose.

Janet: You should tell your doctor.

Kate: I am afraid she will lock me up.

Janet: She can give you an antidepressant. It can help.

Kate: Do you think I might be like that woman who was in the news?

Janet: I can babysit for you if you need some relief.

Kate: So you think this is serious too, don't you?

Looking for reassurance when you feel guilty might make you feel somewhat better in the short term, but it adds to your suffering when you realize that it sometimes upsets or frightens others and ultimately strengthens Worried Voice. Much better is to practice noticing that feelings associated with your thoughts will go away on their own if you just leave them alone.

Doubt

Every time you have an unwanted intrusive thought, you want to know for sure that there is no danger and the intrusion will safely pass. Trying to abolish all doubts and eradicate uncertainty is a significant impediment to reaching an attitude of acceptance. Everyone wants to be absolutely sure that not struggling with the thought is a safe thing to do and that there is no danger in labeling it as a thought, as opposed to an impulse. You want to be certain that the thought is 100 percent not a reflection on your character and that absolutely you will not go crazy or lose control. This is a natural wish. Unfortunately, it is not one that can be satisfied.

The fight for certainty is a major factor in keeping your unwanted intrusive thoughts so intense. And, if you think about it, where else do you demand absolute certainty? Do you put your car up on a lift and have a skilled mechanic check the brakes, steering, and transmission every time you go for a spin? Do you stay off sidewalks because cars sometimes lose control and run over pedestrians? Do you insist that someone taste your food before you eat? Do you ask your kids if they still love you every hour? Of course not!

The problem is that unwanted intrusive thoughts *feel* so threatening. That is because anxious thinking takes over, and the thought—as abhorrent as it might be—*seems* to have a high probability of occurring. And, you might think, even if the probability is fairly low, the consequences of killing someone or throwing a child out the window are so enormous and horrendous that the thought feels threatening and dangerous.

False Comfort: Wise Mind, I need to find some better way to reassure Worried Voice that the thoughts don't matter, but it keeps asking the same question over and over no matter what I say.

Wise Mind: The problem is thinking Worried Voice is reassurable. What-ifs will always come up. Worried Voice has to learn to tolerate that it can't have a 100 percent guarantee. None of us really have certainty about anything.

False Comfort: But when I don't reassure Worried Voice, it gets worse, and it also gets angry at me.

Wise Mind: Tell Worried Voice that you love it, but if you keep reassuring it, it will never learn how to live with uncertainty, and that is something we all have to learn how to do.

Seeking external reassurance is yet another step in the unhelpful fight for certainty. Once again, people seek external reassurance to quell their doubts. Frequently their friends and family provide additional false comfort, just to keep their loved one comfortable in the moment or to get them to stop asking for reassurance. It does not work past a few moments of relief. This kind of exchange is not helpful.

Self: Tell me you are sure that the plane will not crash while you are on it. I keep worrying over and over about it, and it feels like a premonition.

Family member: Don't be silly. I promise I will be fine. I will call you when I get there.

Self: But you can't really be sure. Please don't go. I am getting a message here.

Family member: Planes are safe.

Self: Okay, but you have to call me as soon as you land. I'll be worrying about you the whole time.

Sometimes you get so involved with the need for reassurance that you become addicted to that need. These are the reassurance junkies that we mentioned in chapter 6. If you see yourself as a reassurance junkie, try this approach: Give yourself a weekly "ration" of reassurances (Robbins 2013). Act as if reassurance were very, very expensive, and your budget is tight. Use it only when it seems absolutely necessary. It can be your first step in breaking the reassurance habit.

This is very different from the ordinary sorts of reassurance and encouragement that people ask for, and receive, in the course of their daily lives. Real reassurance happens just once, it works, and the issue is closed. It is not an answer to an unanswerable question or an empty promise.

The Gun Test: Finding Your Own Wise Mind

Because doubts inevitably accompany every step of the six steps, we would like you to explicitly call up your own Wise Mind. Wise Mind is often drowned out by the noise of your other two entangled and struggling voices. Here is one avenue for contacting that part of you that *really knows* what is going on—the one that bought this book and has kept reading, the one who knows the unwanted thoughts are not the *real you,* the unflappable one who knows not to grant more meaning to a thought than it deserves. This thought experiment was inspired by Grayson (2003).

Imagine that you have suddenly been placed in a do-or-die situation. There is a gun to your head, ready to fire, and you get only one guess to answer the question. You cannot know for certain—all you get is your best guess. If you are right, you live; if you are wrong, you die. Do nothing and you die as well. There are no maybes, no hedging, and no time to think about it anymore, nor to ask anyone else. This is it. You get one guess. Now answer the questions:

- Is this just an unwanted intrusive thought or a meaningful message?
- Should I apply the steps and allow the thought to be there?
- Should I turn myself in to the police or the mental hospital, or can I safely let this thought alone?
- Is it my best guess that this will pass if I don't get entangled and don't let False Comfort get involved?
- Should I allow myself to be hijacked by this junk?

If the imaginary stakes are do-or-die, your own Wise Mind will step forward. It might be 51 percent versus 49 percent in terms of certainty, but a part of you really does know what to guess. Most say that they *know* these thoughts are meaningless intrusions, but aren't 100 percent sure—and they wish that they could be certain. The gun test forces them to make that choice.

Urgency

As we have discussed, a feeling of urgency accompanies every unwanted intrusive thought. Giving in to that sense of urgency takes you in a direction that is contrary to the therapeutic attitude of acceptance. We know that each intrusion seems to indicate an emergency (or an emergency in the making), and you need to do something about it immediately. But this is a *false alarm.* When you get bluffed, or tricked, by this false alarm, you will spend your energy trying to turn off the alarm and encounter the effects of paradoxical effort, inadvertently increasing entanglement. Urgency makes you feel that issues need to be addressed now, not later. It makes it hard to pause before labeling, to float above the fray, to accept and allow, and to let time pass. In fact, a feeling of urgency works counter to every essential step for coping with unwanted intrusive thoughts. There is a relationship between being bothered by uncertainty and the feeling of urgency. If something is unclear or uncertain, there is an urgent desire to clear it up now.

Family and friends can start to believe that you are in an emergency too and reinforce the idea that you have to do something now if you seek help from them. They come up with all the things False Comfort has already tried.

Self: I am being bombarded. I don't know if I can hold out any longer. I can't stand these crazy thoughts; I am going to lose my mind. I have to do something *now.*

Friend: Maybe you should take Xanax and lie down for a while.

Self: I don't want to get addicted, and anyway the thoughts just come back.

Friend: Maybe you should pray for inner peace. I will hold your hand. I will stay with you until you feel better.

Self: Do you think I need to go to the hospital?

Friend: I will take you if you can't calm down, but I am sure you will be okay.

Self: I can't make up my mind whether I should go. I feel like I'm missing my chance. Tell me again why you are sure I will be okay?

The most helpful response to the feeling of urgency is to slow down, float above the fray, and practice letting time pass.

Some Helpful Metaphors

Don't feel discouraged if you find it hard to grasp the shift in attitude that underlies the six steps. Here are some stories and metaphors to help illustrate different aspects of this attitude shift. Applying the steps is not so much a set of rules of *what to do* but reminders of *how to be.* The steps are counterintuitive—in other words, they seem at first to be the opposite of the commonsense way of handling unwanted intrusive thoughts. These stories illustrate how doing the opposite of the commonsense way is what actually works (Stoddard, Afari, and Hayes 2014).

The Intruder at the Party

Imagine you are giving a party that is very important to you, and you have invited friends, family, and coworkers—people you really care about. You have gone all-out on the food, including some very expensive shrimp. Everyone seems to be enjoying themselves. Suddenly you notice a scruffy guy you do not recognize. He is at the buffet and is helping himself to shrimp. You politely ask him to leave, but he simply ignores you. You have a choice now. You can confront him, call the police, have him thrown out of the party, and then stand by the door to make sure he does not return. This will immediately make a commotion, interrupt the enjoyment of others, and brand your party the "one when the police came." Or you can allow him to take some shrimp, just ignore him, and go about enjoying the party. Interestingly, no one else seems to mind this intruder as much as you.

This illustrates how labeling and allowing (the opposite of fighting) changes perspective. Pay attention to what really matters. Steps one and two of the six steps to reduce distress over a thought require that you get the situation labeled correctly. When you label and understand that this scruffy guy is "just taking shrimp," it allows you to realize that you have the option of not doing anything. There is no danger—although perhaps some irritation—and that option might be preferable to making a huge fuss and spoiling your party. In a similar manner, when you label a thought—no matter how repugnant—as "just a thought," you give yourself the option of safely choosing to leave it alone. You are bigger than a thought, any thought, and it requires no control. You can then move toward the attitude of acceptance embodied in step 3.

Whack-a-Mole

Imagine that you are at an amusement park and spot the Whacka-Mole game. There is a huge stuffed panda bear you would like to win. You put down your money and stand alert for the start bell. You pick up your mallet and discover, just as the clanging starts, that the mallet is tied down by a six-inch cord, and there is no way to reach any of the moles as they pop up and down. Your score is clearly going to be zero. You have a choice now. You can get angry, feel cheated, be embarrassed, fight to tear your mallet off the cord—or you can laugh at the absurdity of the whole situation.

Initial reactions here might be frustration, anger, embarrassment, or even anxiety. But by letting go and accepting, you can make something that seemed important (getting the panda bear) feel trivial and even funny. This is an illustration of step 3, accepting and allowing.

Don't Dignify the Question

The president is having a press conference. Suddenly someone jumps up and shouts, "Is it true that you are having an affair with your personal secretary?" He has a few options now. He can protest loudly, "Do not be ridiculous!" and the papers will read, "President denies affair with secretary." Or he can have the reporter thrown out: "President ejects reporter who asks about his affair with secretary." Or he can look straight at the reporter, make it clear he heard the question, and then pivot to "Next question please." He can refuse to dignify the question with a response (Papantonio 2013).

This illustrates that there are some no-win situations in which any engagement will result in additional entanglement. An unwanted intrusive thought is one of those situations. No matter how obviously it seems to call for argument, rejection, or reaction, getting involved is not advised. Unwanted intrusive thoughts do not deserve the dignity of a response. This is another way to understand the meaning of acceptance in step 3.

The Waterfall

You are sitting comfortably and peacefully on a lawn chair on a ledge behind a waterfall. You can feel a little light spray, but you are perfectly safe. As you watch the water cascading in front of you, you can see some debris from upstream, and something goes by that looks like it might be valuable. But you know if you reach for it, you will have to forgo the pleasure of this experience, strain yourself to catch it, and it might not be of any worth at all. You might even lose your footing. So you just watch it go by.

This illustrates that the natural flow of the mind has debris that may sometimes feel important, but is not worth examining. In these cases, letting it go by is the best strategy. Not every thought we think is important or worth retrieving. Floating behind the waterfall and just observing is a way of understanding step 4, float and feel.

Mud on the Windshield

You are driving on a country road with large puddles from a recent rain, and you are running late for an appointment. A splat of mud lands on your windshield, and there is a disgusting dead bug in the middle of it. You have a choice now. You could put on the old windshield wiper, but it will just spread mud and bug parts all over the windshield. You can stop by the side of the road, get a rag, and spend time cleaning it off—and be even later for your appointment. Or you can just keep driving. You realize that you have a safe view of the road through and around the dirt, even though the mess is somewhat irritating. So you continue to drive. As the sun hits the windshield, it dries the mud, the wind flicks it off, and your windshield is almost clean by the time you arrive.

This metaphor illustrates that sometimes doing nothing, floating past an intrusion, just letting it remain, is the most effective way to be. This is a way of understanding the principles embodied in steps 3, 4, and 5—accept and allow, float and feel, and let time pass.

Noisy Neighbors

You are on your back porch reading, and you hear neighbors arguing with each other in angry voices. They do this all the time. You neither try to figure out what they are arguing about, nor do you go over and get involved. You just wait it out patiently and go back to your reading. They eventually stop.

Headache

You have a headache. You still go to work, and at some point during the day, you notice that the headache has gone away. You did not do anything to make it go away. Sometimes just continuing on with your everyday activity is an effective way to not struggle with an issue while you simply let time pass.

These stories are ways of showing that everyday life is filled with examples of the suggestions outlined in the six steps to reduce stress over a thought. Continuing what you do while allowing time to pass is a way to let your mind and body relax by itself, naturally.

You now have an attitude and strategy for better dealing with unwanted intrusive thoughts that ambush you out of the blue. This strategy and attitude encourage a new perspective and eventually will significantly reduce your distress. It will take practice to avoid the anxiety traps and hijackings, and to learn these new ways. But please don't lose hope: this approach has been helpful for hundreds of people like you, who initially felt overwhelmed and at wit's end. You have already learned so much and made such significant changes. The next chapter introduces a plan of deliberate actions that can develop new brain circuitry so unwanted thoughts lose their power and stop bothering you at all.

CHAPTER 8

Getting Over Unwanted Thoughts for Good

Our goal is to change the way your brain works. This will result in changing how unwanted thoughts feel so eventually they will stop bothering you. What you have learned by now is that your usual and customary way of coping with unwanted intrusive thoughts fails to do that. In fact, it does the opposite and keeps your brain, your body, and your thoughts locked into their present cycle. We have explained how the attitude of acceptance is what opens the door for changes to occur, and in this chapter we lay out a program of deliberate actions to enable this to happen.

There is widespread agreement that the most effective way to change your brain and get over your unwanted intrusive thoughts is—believe it or not—to allow yourself to think your frightening thoughts on purpose. In other words, to expose yourself to the thoughts *intentionally,* while practicing new and better ways to manage your reactions. When you take charge of the experience instead of being bombarded by it, you rewire your brain and create lasting changes. This is called *exposure work.*

The attitude of acceptance is essential to gaining the most benefit from exposure work. In fact, exposure work without acceptance is just a recipe for misery and is ineffective. Being willing to be uncomfortable is important, but if you also understand how exposure works, it may give you additional motivation and courage. This will set the foundation for optimizing practice.

Helpful Fact: Exposure is the active therapeutic ingredient for overcoming anxiety.

Get Uncomfortable on Purpose

Why should you make yourself more uncomfortable on purpose? Aren't you reading this book in the hopes of becoming *less* uncomfortable?

The answer is that we want you to do better than just feel more comfortable. Our ultimate goal is to help you end your suffering. That means taking a larger perspective and agreeing to put up with more discomfort in the present so you can suffer less in the future. The way to the other side of troubled water is through it since there is no effective way to run around it. And we know that to rewire the brain, we have to activate fears to change them. The good news is that practicing isn't as frightening as you might imagine.

Remember that your amygdala is just an alarm system. Think of it like an infant—it has no subtlety or words—so you can't teach it new information by using words. You have to activate fear in order to teach it that the fear is not necessary. When you actively and willingly trigger the fear pathway, you allow your brain to be rewired. That allows fear to decrease and for the adoption of the attitude of acceptance.

By now you have learned a great deal about how your brain and your body—in conjunction with your three inner voices, Worried Voice, False Comfort, and Wise Mind—create and continue to power your unwanted intrusive thoughts. Exposure is the opportunity to change the ways those characters interact. Exposure gives you the opportunity to put in effect the information you have already learned. Exposure is the way to turn your learning from "knowing in your head" to "knowing in your heart, brain, and body." *Exposure is the way to find and trust your own Wise Mind.* Exposure is the opportunity to train your brain to change.

You can never become fluent in a foreign language by only reading books on vocabulary and grammar. You need to tolerate awkwardness and discomfort, and practice speaking the new language.

In exactly the same way, you will learn best how to overcome unwanted intrusive thoughts by intentionally provoking them and coping with them while your brain and body are reacting.
Worried Voice: Oh, no! I can't imagine that I'll be able to intentionally think my awful thoughts. What if it makes me sick? Or makes me worse? Or what if I can't handle it and lose control?

False Comfort: Come on; I'll help you. We'll make sure you are okay and don't do anything that sends you over the edge.

Worried Voice: Over the edge! Oh no! Do you think I might lose my mind doing this exposure stuff? How will you make sure I don't go over the edge?

False Comfort: No, I think you will be fine. But all your worrying is starting to get to me. Why don't you just think about something else?

Worried Voice: How can I think about something else when I'm supposed to think the thought? Do you think I might actually do what goes through my mind? That would be terrible!

Wise Mind: Both of you would do better by getting closer to the present. Do yourself a favor and listen to yourselves. Do either of you think you are helpful? We are being offered a path that has been helpful to others and seems like it might be helpful to us. I am willing to try something new as the old ways surely do not work. I would like to try it, and I hope you two can figure out a way to go along as well. You are just going to need a little faith.

If the content of each intrusive thought is meaningless, you might be wondering why we ask you to think those particular thoughts. It is because your *attitude* and *sensitivity* toward these thoughts are what you are aiming to change. There is no better way to do that than to face precisely the worst thoughts you can come up with. If you avoid the thoughts that trigger you the most, you give them even more power. If you compromise and invoke anything less than the real thing, you are forgetting that thoughts—*any* thoughts—are just thoughts.

Changing Your Brain: How Extinction Works

There are two ways to explain how your brain learns to become less fearful as a result of exposure. One is called *emotional processing,* and the other is called *inhibitory learning.* Both theories are supported by brain research, so we are going to give you a short explanation of both.

Emotional Processing Explained

Emotional-processing theory (Foa and Kozak 1986) states that your brain develops false *fearful memory structures* that keep your fears alive. When you consistently avoid or run away from thoughts that trigger these memory structures, you never learn that they are incorrect and that your thought isn't really dangerous. As a result of keeping away from the triggers, they remain part of your brain for very long periods of time. You don't have the chance to habituate—or get used to—the thought because your false brain structures tell you they are dangerous and you should keep away.

This theory explains why actively inviting the thoughts *along with the anxiety* creates *corrective emotional processing* so fearful memory structures in your brain become accurate. Real experience allows false fear memories to be emotionally processed, and your fear will then be erased. But there are two important requirements.

The first is that corrective emotional processing only occurs in the presence of fear since the fear is what allows the memory structures in the brain to change. The technical term is "exposure plus activation." Any exposure that activates anxiety brings the false fear structures into play, and they change as a result of seeing that nothing dangerous (as opposed to frightening) really happens.

The second requirement is that you keep in contact with your triggering thoughts until your anxiety goes away or at least calms down considerably. This allows your brain to get used to the thought and habituate to it. You get maximum therapeutic benefits from exposures that are long enough for this to happen.

Emotional processing theory makes it very clear why avoiding the thought won't work. Avoidance keeps you experiencing the thought as dangerous or intolerable, and that sets the stage to retrigger your amygdala. Worried Voice plays the part of the false (but powerful) fear structures in your brain. But the voice of False Comfort is the voice that represents avoidance and distraction, and both of those interfere with emotional processing.

Inhibitory Learning Explained

Another more recent model explains the therapeutic benefits of exposure in a slightly different way. The inhibitory-learning model (Craske et al. 2008) of exposure says that people don't really unlearn old, fearful responses. Instead, what happens is that new pathways are created in the brain that compete with the old, fearful response. The more new pathways that are created, the greater the chance that a nonfearful path will be chosen. If you practice it enough, you create many nonfearful responses that *inhibit* the scary one. A nonfearful response then becomes the default response, and you are no longer afraid.

Imagine that your fearful response is the main road going through your town. And imagine that a planned highway is the new reaction. If a highway is built right next to the road, the highway will become used more and more until the road is barely used. The road still exists, but it handles less and less traffic as people get used to the convenience of the highway. Exposure work creates the new highway.

Inhibitory learning is new learning. Even if you don't entirely habituate to (become completely okay with) whatever you are trying to get used to, your new pathways are being formed. You do best when you practice frequently, in many different situations, under a variety of conditions. If we go back to the model of the highway, frequent and varied practice helps to create more on and off-ramps for the highway. It will be easier to get on and off, and you will use it more frequently.

This way of looking at exposure also explains a distressing phenomenon that you have surely experienced. Sometimes, for no apparent reason, something that has stopped upsetting you some time ago can occasionally trigger a bolt of anxiety. Now we know that the fearful path is still there, but is hardly ever used. So you have to be prepared for anxiety to occasionally show up. It is actually more likely to happen when your mind is stickier, such as when you are fatigued or stressed by something else. What it means is that you are temporarily stickier, not that the learning you have already done is lost.

What is most important about exposure is that you stay in contact with what frightens you until the feelings seem more manageable. They don't have to go away, but you should stay long enough so they seem a little more tolerable. You might say that your description of the fearful feelings goes from "They are so uncomfortable that I find them intolerable" to "They are uncomfortable but tolerable." The goal is to feel that you can tolerate the anxiety better, as opposed to eliminating it completely. There is a lot of evidence to suggest that being able and willing to *tolerate* anxiety, as opposed to *eliminating* anxiety, actually results in more durable and long-term recovery.

In other words, it is your inability to tolerate your unwanted intrusive thoughts that keeps them going. That inability keeps your brain using the old, fear-provoking pathways and prevents new ones from being created.

If unwanted intrusive thoughts just don't matter because you have less fear of them and you are able to tolerate them much better, they then fade out on their own. New, nonfearful pathways in your brain are utilized and strengthened.

Both theories have one very important aspect in common: the ingredient for getting over your fears is—paradoxical as it might seem—allowing yourself to experience them.

Planned Practice vs. Incidental Practice

In chapter 7 ("How to Handle Thoughts When They Happen"), we presented detailed steps to make the most of each unwanted intrusive thought as it occurred. That is *incidental practice:* making the most of an intrusion that seems to come out of the blue. It is practice you get to do when thoughts happen. But you can speed your recovery by deliberately increasing the opportunities to create new brain pathways.

Planned practice occurs when you intentionally expose yourself to your triggers, or intentionally have the unwanted intrusive thoughts that set off your fear alarm system. You goal is to focus on what is happening inside you so you can practice reacting to the false alarms in new and more helpful ways, so you can teach your brain.

For the time that you are actually engaged in planned practice, *you want to be anxious!* Experiencing anxiety helps you practice engaging the paradoxical attitude of acceptance while your brain and body are yelling, "Danger! Get away from here! Avoid!" This is a hard task, and it requires willingness to be uncomfortable. You are willingly allowing yourself to stay where you want to avoid, allowing uncertainty to remain when your inner voices are begging for certainty and intentionally allowing the feeling that seems so dangerous. We are asking you to react without urgency as your Worried Voice is screaming at you to "do something!" We are asking you to out-bluff anxiety, to refuse to be hijacked, and to stand up to the bullies in your mind.

Once again, consider the alternative: to continue the enormous avoidance efforts you have already expended—and continue to expend—that don't actually provide help and just maintain your suffering.

Five A's for Optimal Practice

You will get the most out of planned practice if you can keep certain principles in mind as you grapple with unwanted intrusive thoughts. Remember that anxiety will be working hard to trick you into believing that your thoughts really do represent all the upsetting myths that were debunked in chapter 3 ("What Thoughts Mean: Myths and Facts"). In fact, this might be an excellent time to review that chapter, since your Worried Voice might very well be repeating every one of those myths.

Here are the five A's, which we will explain in more detail.

1.	Attitude of acceptance
2.	Assign accurate assessment
3.	Active allowance of awareness and affect
4.	Avoid avoidances (always attempt approach)
5.	Action: advance activities anyway

Attitude of Acceptance

In chapter 7, we explained how to apply the attitude of acceptance to each unwanted intrusive thought as it pops up. Now we are asking you to expand that attitude toward your planned exposure practice. Remember that acceptance is the opposite of fighting with the feeling or fleeing from the thought, and it is part of the paradoxical nature of anxiety that accepting the feelings and the thoughts is the most efficient way to get rid of them.

Assign Accurate Assessment

Remember that you are practicing with unwanted intrusive thoughts. They are thoughts, just thoughts, and only thoughts. They might feel different from many of your other thoughts, but that doesn't change the fact that they are only thoughts. Despite the commentary that anxiety is feeding you, intrusive thoughts are not impulses, indications of your character, nor messages from you "inner self" that something awful happened or is about to happen.

Helpful Fact: Anxiety tries to convince you that intrusive thoughts have a special meaning. Part of beating anxious thinking is refusing to be taken in by this misleading message.

Your job is to stay with the label—that this is an unwanted intrusive thought and not an issue—and trust your assessment, despite the doubts and what-ifs that are sure to surface. Remember that your amygdala has sounded its false alarm, and so the thoughts "feel" different—they feel dangerous. Remember that feelings aren't facts and that anxiety's role is to trick you into running away from the thoughts and pushing away the feelings. You know this is an intrusive thought by the way it feels and the way it acts. It *feels* awful and contains an urgent sense to get rid of it. And it acts like a bad penny. It shows up again and again.

Active Allowance of Awareness and Affect

While you are practicing exposure to unwanted intrusive thoughts, your goal is to allow all thoughts and feelings into awareness. (The word "affect" is the term that psychologists use to describe emotions.) This is the ultimate goal that you are aiming for, but it's not something that you should expect to obtain right away, so don't get upset at yourself when—not if—you fall short.

Keep in mind that the more of your emotions and thoughts you can keep in awareness, the more effective your exposure will be in producing habituation and inhibitory learning. Actively allowing awareness makes your planned practice work better and will help you avoid some of the pitfalls that anxiety brings.

Worried Voice: I'll never be able to allow awareness. All the bad things that can happen fill up my mind. I'm a failure.

False Comfort: I know you can try harder! Just a little more discipline and less mollycoddling will do it.

Worried Voice: But I try as hard as I can. I can't do it any better! I can't stand it.

Wise Mind: We can be both disciplined and gentle with ourselves. Our job is to allow awareness of all we can, and also to gently, tenderly, and kindly bring ourselves back to that task when we become distracted. Our mind naturally wanders off. That is okay. Discipline and gentleness: that's the most productive approach.

Avoid Avoidances (Always-Attempt Approach)

Optimal practice embraces the principle that anxiety is maintained by avoidance, and overcoming anxiety means moving to areas of greater discomfort. Avoiding avoidances is the principle that describes this approach.

Remember that the *purpose* of planned practice is to generate anxiety by doing what is required to trigger your amygdala. The amygdala only learns not to be afraid when the fear pathways are activated. Repeated clanging of the alarm response sets the stage for emotional processing, inhibitory learning, and for your brain to "rewire" itself so the thought no longer sounds the alarm. Avoidance blocks learning.

Always attempting to approach the trigger will give you an overall direction to head when you are in the midst of practicing. If you are in the midst of a planned practice and you aren't sure whether you should stay with the thought or distract yourself in some way, the *always-attempt approach* will guide you toward staying with the thought and discourage you from looking for a distraction. If, during a planned practice, you have the thought that this will interfere with your work later and so you should cut it short, this principle will encourage you to stay with the task and not avoid it because of some future concern.

Avoidances can be both behavioral as well as mental. If you cancel a lunch with a woman who often triggers unwanted intrusive thoughts that you might be gay or you miss church services because of the fearful thought that you might yell out blasphemy, those are behavioral avoidances. And avoidance can be much subtler than that. You might go to church and insist on sitting in the last row so you can quickly and easily leave the church "just in case" the thoughts start up. Or you might go to lunch with the woman but talk incessantly and barely look at her. That is a form of avoidance as well.

Additionally, avoidances can be purely mental. Avoidances occur when False Comfort tries to quiet Worried Voice. In these cases, you are trying to avoid the anxious feeling with internal dialogue. But, as you know, False Comfort is *always* followed by another round of Worried Voice.

In general, all avoidances reinforce and empower your unwanted intrusive thoughts. It is the exact opposite of what we want. We want your intrusions to become less powerful and you to be less and less susceptible to their messages.

Action: Advance Activities Anyway

This principle reminds you to return to your task at hand after your planned practice session as well as after each intrusive thought that seems to come from out of the blue. Remember that your goal is to achieve a new way to relate to your thoughts that is unentangled and free of struggle. When you deliberately invite these thoughts, you do not give them the power to waylay your life.

One way to achieve this is to continue doing the things you were doing prior to the thoughts. As we have mentioned in the previous chapter, unwanted intrusive thoughts can be compared to internal bullies. The most effective anti-bully activity is to refuse to let them change your daily activities. If you don't, then you are giving power to the bully's message. You can expect to feel afraid (there's your amygdala again), but your most therapeutic reaction is to continue with your life and ignore the apparent message.

The Nitty Gritty of Planned Practice

Now we are going to explain some of the specific ways that you can practice on your own that will encourage the most therapeutic benefits of exposure. This might be a good time to review the six steps explained in the previous chapter.

Go at Your Own Pace

The overarching rule is that self-directed exposure work must feel manageable. You will make the most progress if you allow yourself permission to go at your own pace. Manageable does not mean comfortable since little anxiety reduction is learned by a comfortable brain. There is no set "speed limit" for how fast and how intensely you should work. There is no magic level of anxiety that is optimal. What feels manageable one day might feel much too difficult—or perhaps too easy—the next. The general principle is that you should strive to work at a level that feels manageable but is still a stretch or a challenge. This may vary from day to day, as your level of sensitization, or the "stickiness" of your mind, goes up and down. In general, the faster the pace, the more rapid the learning. But if you go so fast that you can't apply the five A's, then you might be just sounding the alarm and not learning anything helpful.

Think the Thought—the Worst Thought—but with a Twist

Since the thought frightens or disgusts you, one of the best ways to practice is to invite the thought to enter your awareness in a slightly altered way. Stay connected to the thought while accepting and allowing the feeling to remain. Here are some ways that you can practice having your most uncomfortable thoughts with a bit of change. And remember, humor is your best ally during practice.

- Sing the thought to the tune of "Happy Birthday" or "Twinkle, Twinkle, Little Star."
- Write the thought over and over.
- Make a poem of the thought.
- Songify the thought (the app is free).
- Draw or paint the thought.
- Record the thought and play it back.
- Elaborate the thought into a full script with a terrible ending. *Read it over and over.*
- Write the thought on sticky notes and paste them all over the house (the mirror, the fridge, your purse).
- Translate the thought to another language.
- Say the words backward.
- Carry the written thought around in your pocket or tucked inside your clothing.
- Stand in front of a mirror and speak the thought out loud, *over and over.*
- Try to make the thought even worse—to the point of absurdity.
- Add the phrase *I am having the thought that ...* to the thought, or

I am seeing the image of ... to the image, and repeat it on each step as you go up and down the stairs in your home or any time you encounter stairs.

Helpful Fact: Humor goes a long way to making practice more manageable.

Let us listen in on a dialogue.
Worried Voice: Are you serious? Deliberately make myself anxious when I am not? I suffer enough!

False Comfort: Wise Mind says this is the best way to feel better. It is like having to hurt a bit to get an injection, but the medication is worth it. We will likely be more anxious at first, and that is how change happens. Our brain needs to be activated to learn a new way. It should be okay.

Worried Voice: But what if it isn't? What if I just make myself worse?

False Comfort: We can always fall back on the old ways, like gritting our teeth and holding our breath and avoiding stuff, even though it doesn't really work.

Wise Mind: This kind of work demands a leap of faith. Many others have taken this leap. Actually, being willing to take the risk is exactly the attitude that makes this whole thing effective. It is the willingness that is the key. The unwanted intrusive thought that is wanted and deliberately sought becomes a passing thought of no consequence.

Avoid Getting Caught Up in Content

There are some phrases that you can say to yourself as a way of helping you disentangle from the content of your intrusive thought. Here is a list that others have found helpful. You might think of some others as well.

- *That's a thought.*
- *Yes, damned if I can't know that.*
- *Any thought can be tolerated, even that one.*

- *Nothing is certain, so I will get used to it.*
- *I can think of something worse.*
- Change what-if to what-is: move from thinking to sensing. For example, instead of responding to a what-if question, pivot your attention gently over to your senses: what can you hear, see, smell right *now* here in the moment? What does your body feel like? Notice without judgment or struggle.

Examples of Planned Practice

It is sometimes hard to get the flavor of planned practicing by describing each element separately. For that reason, we present three separate scenarios involving planned practice in real life.

"My son was in a car accident."

A young mother was plagued by unwanted intrusive thoughts and images that her son had been in a car accident. She was texting him many times a day to reassure herself that her thoughts were not omens or predictions, or that somehow they were the product of a mother's "intuition."

After education about intrusive thoughts—what they mean and don't mean—and an understanding that her efforts to avoid the thoughts were what was keeping them going, she agreed to begin planned practice. She was instructed to sing a new song "Johnny Is Dead by the Side of the Road" to the tune of "Twinkle, Twinkle, Little Star"—over and over, and to imagine a picture of him crumpled outside a crushed car at the same time. She was to do this not just when she had the urge to text him, but when she was showering, cooking, making the beds, vacuuming, shopping, eating, and every time she picked up a phone, computer, or other electronic device.

At first this was very difficult for her, but surprisingly quickly, it was boring, and shortly thereafter, it felt absurd to be upset by the song. She had defeated the thoughts by deliberately inviting them to bother her.

"What If I Kill Myself? I Don't Want to Die!"

A middle-aged man who lived alone kept having the profoundly disturbing and, to him, absurd thought that he might hang himself against his own wishes. This began after a celebrity had in fact done so, stunning and upsetting everyone. After sufficient psychoeducation, he was encouraged to carry around a rope so he would not forget to practice having the thought *I could hang myself in a moment of impulse* many times a day. He also placed a rope in his car and in his bathroom hanging from the shower rod. When he noticed his own False Comfort voice trying to reassure him with "But you are a happy man! You would never do that!" he was instructed to add "Nothing is impossible" and then to be willing to have the disturbing thought again on purpose. After a while, the ropes no longer made him upset.

"I might oversleep."

A woman kept herself awake for hours every night, trying to respond to the unwanted intrusive thought *I have to make sure my alarm clock is set properly.* She would alternate between actually checking the clock and dealing with the returning thought that she had not set it properly. Usually she could refrain from more clock checking but not from more memory checking. She would carefully think back over her memory, checking it to make sure she clearly remembered doing it. She lay for hours trying to check her memories, reassuring herself and berating herself for the absurdity of the situation.

She was instructed to tell herself *I invite the thought that I may not have set the alarm properly.* She began to sing the thought (including the elaborated story that she might be late to work) to "Lullaby and Goodnight." She was not to attempt to fall asleep, but just lie in bed resting and allowing the unwanted thought. She got bored. She fell asleep after twenty minutes of planned practice. The struggle was over.

It came back as a kind of jolt as she lay in bed, particularly when she was stressed by a work or family issue, but she knew not to fight the thought or try to make it go away. And it became a familiar passing thought on her way to sleep.

Eventually you will discover that the thoughts you invite in—with acceptance, deliberateness, and willingness—change how they feel and how they act. They lose their power to frighten you, disgust you, upset you, or even deter you from doing whatever you wish. They lose their illusion of being meaningful and important. You feel more free.

When you do these planned exposures, you are disentangling from them and disempowering them with your attitude of acceptance. The more you practice, the faster this happens. You take back control by refusing to control, and you regain composure and self-respect by allowing the natural course of your mind to proceed. You deprive the thoughts of the fuel of paradoxical effort, and they dwindle in importance and, eventually, in strength. Recovery occurs when it no longer matters whether the thoughts happen or not.

In this chapter, we have discussed the most potent way to get over unwanted intrusive thoughts so they no longer cause you distress. In the next chapter, we address the best way to think about recovery, what it is, and how to maintain it.

CHAPTER 9

What Does Recovery Mean?

In this chapter, we address recovery—what recovery is and how it is maintained. You may notice we are not using the word "cure," which implies you had symptoms of an illness and now the illness is gone. We do this for a specific reason: unlike with an illness, the absence of symptoms is not a sufficient definition of recovery.

Relief from the struggle with unwanted intrusive thoughts is certainly part of our achievable goals for you, but we are actually suggesting something even more ambitious. We want you to do more than simply have the thoughts stop bothering you. We are aiming for an *inoculation* for the future as well—so when intrusive thoughts occur once again (and you will remember, we all have them, and everyone can expect to experience them from time to time), you will be able to handle them so they do not cause a problem, do not get sticky and repetitive, and do not start that familiar internal dialogue that makes them frightening, disgusting, or shameful.

You have certainly come a long way in your recovery, and we congratulate you! You have learned a lot about what thoughts mean and what they don't mean, and you have done a lot of practice to change your automatic reactions to your unwanted intrusive thoughts. Let's review what you will carry forward from here.

There are three aspects of this inoculation that we have been addressing throughout this book. The first is a knowledge of how thoughts affect feelings and the understanding that your thoughts—and, in fact, any thoughts—have the capacity to automatically trigger your alarm system. The second is enhancing your ability to slow down so you are able to better observe the flow of thoughts. And the third is gaining a gentler, nonjudgmental, and more accepting relationship with your mind. The result is that you are able to accept and allow all your thoughts, along with the automatic feelings that come with them.

When you started this book, if you had heard that our goal was to change your relationship to your thoughts, you might have had an objection that went something like this:

Worried Voice: I don't just want to change my relationship with those awful thoughts. I want them to go away and never come back!

False Comfort: These people must know what they are doing. They seem to be saying that we have to accept, that we will be tortured, and that we will learn how to deal with it.

Worried Voice: That is a raw deal.

False Comfort: Maybe hypnosis would work.

But you are at a point now where you can also access your Wise Mind. This is the part of you that has learned that accepting and allowing these thoughts is the path toward training your brain to stop fighting them. You have practiced a change of attitude when unwanted thoughts showed up, and you have deliberately invoked these thoughts in order to practice this Wise Mind response.

Wise Mind: No, hang in there, guys. Here is the actual deal. *If the thoughts really don't matter to us, they actually stop coming!* Because we have stopped fueling them with our disgust, fear, anger, and shame. The path to the other side of the storm where all is calm is through it. We can't outrun it or circle around it. But if we walk forward through it, it does not take long to pass. We have the same goal: to not be bombarded by intrusive thoughts we don't want.

We say that Wise Mind is right, and here is why: You were sensitized to the thoughts, and so you dreaded them, braced for them, and worried about their recurrence. You avoided situations that might trigger them.

We call this anticipatory anxiety. You can think of it as the what-if about the what-if. Anticipatory anxiety causes you to project into the future in an attempt to prepare yourself for the next unwanted intrusive thought. You hope they do not come, and you are upset when they do. You are involved in a struggle with your mind.

The result is that you keep oriented toward the future, pay very little attention to the present, and keep your body and mind sensitized. You remain vigilant, with your body poised to react. It keeps Worried Voice and False Comfort in constant conversation. It promotes stickiness in your mind. But most importantly, it keeps the unwanted intrusive thoughts coming! Defending against thoughts brings them to the foreground: your brain automatically re-creates them and continues the cycle.

Starting the Cycle of Recovery

You are now starting to experience intrusive thoughts in a new way. Your beliefs about them are totally different. You think that they are silly, unavoidable blips of your mind, holding no meaning, warning, or power. Pretty soon it becomes boring and unnecessary to be on alert for them. It would be like waiting with bated breath for something ordinary and expected to happen. Like waiting for paint to dry or for a clock to tick the next tick. You would naturally turn your attention to more interesting things, like whatever else you are thinking about or doing. Ordinary things like work, fun, or lunch. You could pay attention to other, more interesting thoughts and feelings. You would be free to experience the world around you.

This lowers overall sensitization, tension, and arousal. This happens quite naturally, without effort or intention. It is not a technique. It just feels normal as this happens: *your mind simply becomes less sticky.* Intrusive thoughts stop having a whoosh attached to them. They may still have the same content, but they feel different. And then they become passing thoughts. They come and go easily. Your worry about them reduces. Your sensitization goes down. The cycle continues. And then they just peter out, on their own, without any help from you. This is the fear-reducing cycle we presented in chapter 5. It ends disturbing, stuck, unwanted intrusive thoughts. They are only passing thoughts.

Worried Voice: I have tried and tried to accept, and then when I check to see if it is working, the thoughts just keep coming back and bothering me. Acceptance just doesn't work for me.

Wise Mind: It is tricky. Acceptance is an attitude for allowing the thoughts and not a technique for stopping them. If you are checking to see if it is working, then you don't actually have the attitude. It is like you have the words but not the music. Acceptance is when you actually don't care whether the thoughts are there or not because they are not important or worthy of attention and because they do not matter. This attitude is what starts the cycle of recovery: reducing anticipatory anxiety, reducing the need for any kind of avoidance, and cultivating a basic okayness with your own mind. This down-regulating results in less stickiness and starts happening on its own once paradoxical effort and entanglement have stopped.

Worried Voice: But how do I make it happen?

Wise Mind: It is not something you do actively; it is passive, like falling asleep or allowing an ant to crawl down your arm without doing anything at all. It involves trusting the process—trusting that there is no hurry, trusting that there is no need for action, trusting when there is uncertainty, and trusting me, the wise part of you.

Stickiness takes some time to go away because it is biologically based and bodies and brains need some adapting time. Sometimes the cycle of recovery takes longer than you wish, but it will happen as you continue to have the attitude that the thoughts do not really matter and there is no need to be on the alert for them. So patiently letting time pass while the body and brain heal themselves is part of the cycle of recovery.

Setback

We like to use the term "setback" instead of "relapse" for the return of unwanted intrusive thoughts. That is because unwanted intrusive thoughts pretty much always return at some point, and we want you to expect them and greet them as a chance to practice accepting them with the right therapeutic attitude.

When you know that intrusive thoughts are likely to return, you are less likely to fall back on old ways of reacting. This can include shock, annoyance, and anger, which then escalate the problem. Part of your job is to remember that thoughts can return at any time, from weeks to years or even decades after they have petered out. But unless you lead an utterly charmed life with no stress, conflict, nights of poor sleep, and no excitement, change, or boredom, there will be a time when the brain just becomes temporarily sticky and old pathways in the brain circuitry are accidentally reactivated.

Setback can happen with meaningless stress like too much caffeine, a cold virus, or bad news from the dentist. Or it can happen when you are dealing with something in your life that is an ongoing issue, like a conflict at work. It may even happen at good times, like if you finally get to have a vacation, you are sitting on the beach perfectly relaxed, and an intrusive thought surprises you. You get mad at it *(Not now!),* while Worried Voice and False Comfort start up their dialogue again after months of absence.

If you do not expect this, then the natural responses to the unwelcome return of thoughts are (1) demoralization *(Oh no, not this again),* (2) anger *(I was sold a bill of goods,* or *Why me?),* (3) fear *(I must be really a sick or bad person),* or (4) hopelessness *(That method works for some people but not for me; it is hopeless for me).*

If you understand that this temporary return of thoughts tends to happen to everyone in recovery, then it is far easier to greet it as an opportunity to practice the attitudes and anti-avoidance skills that may have become rusty over time. In fact, it is actually helpful for it to happen sooner rather than later, so when you have a return of some unwanted intrusions, you don't have to read the whole book again and can just thumb through some reminders. Sometimes the thoughts that return are exactly the same old thoughts. Sometimes they are a slightly altered version of the same thoughts. Sometimes they have morphed into something completely different in content ... but the telltale sign will be there. Remember, it is not the content but how the thoughts and images act and feel (and your instant desire to push them away or get entangled with them) that marks them as unwanted intrusive thoughts.

Worried Voice: I used to worry that I could be a pedophile, and I got over it. I was fine for months. But now suddenly I am plagued with the thought that I could have Lou Gehrig's disease. What a horrible way to go. I hate this.

False Comfort: I know a good neurologist. I will make an appointment.

Worried Voice: I already went to one. She said I have no signs.

False Comfort: Maybe a second opinion would put your mind at ease?

Worried Voice: She said I am almost certainly just anxious, but she could give me an MRI. I have been on WebMD, the Mayo Clinic website, and an ALS chat group to see if I should get one.

Wise Mind: Let me step in here before you embark on a huge medical work-up. Do you recognize what is happening here? Is this thought acting and feeling like the pedophilia ones? Does it keep coming back? Are you getting entangled? Do you need to take a step back, slow down, and get this labeled?

Worried Voice: OH NO! IT'S BACK!

Wise Mind: Do you remember that *we were hoping for a chance to practice* what we have learned about how to handle unwanted intrusive thoughts? This is the chance.

False Comfort: I think we should read the book again.

Wise Mind: Not a bad idea. Everyone forgets the details.

So a healthy way to regard setbacks, no matter when they happen, is that they are to be expected and that they are opportunities to practice what you have already learned about approaching the attitude of acceptance. Intrusive thoughts do not have to usher in another period of suffering and struggle. Often, it takes a bit of self-observation and some words from your Wise Mind to realize that your thoughts are just other examples of unwanted intrusive thoughts not worth exploring or getting entangled with. Here is a question to ask yourself if you notice you are worrying or preoccupied with something unwelcome that keeps intruding, bothering you, and repeating: *What would wise mind say?*

As you know by now, recovery is actually an attitude—a willingness to have whatever thoughts happen to cross your mind, for however long they happen to stay, and whatever they are about. It is a set of beliefs about thoughts: that thoughts are just thoughts and they are not warnings, messages, moral acts, or facts. It is a set of beliefs about your own thoughts: that they are outcroppings of a sticky mind, the opposite of your values and wishes, and not worthy of attention. And it is a way of relating to unwanted intrusive thoughts that is un-entangled, nonjudgmental, and effortless. These attitudes and beliefs leave you inoculated for the future. And when it no longer matters whether the thoughts happen, they then have no fuel, and they fade away.

Congratulations

Congratulations for reading this whole book and for beginning your journey to full recovery. When the intrusion of an unwanted thought no longer activates an internal dialogue; no longer requires effort, action, or avoidance; and just simply does not matter; and when you no longer dread them or even care about them; you are free.

If You Want More

Finally, if you found this book applies to you and it was helpful, you may be interested in following up this work with additional professional help. Below are some websites with directories of local therapists who are trained to treat unwanted intrusive thoughts and for whom the ideas and suggestions of this book are familiar. Unfortunately, not just any therapist or person who claims to treat "anxiety" or unwanted thoughts may be as specialized as you are seeking.

Anxiety and Depression Association of America:

http://www.adaa.org

International OCD Foundation:
http://www.iocdf.org

Association for Behavioral and Cognitive
 Therapies:
http://www.abct.org

CHAPTER 10

When to Seek Professional Help

So far, we have been talking about intrusive thoughts that are frightening but not at all dangerous. They might be frustrating, humiliating, or even shameful, but they are all events that exist only in your mind. Despite your enormous concerns, you are not likely to do the things you think about. As we mentioned, they are the product of *over-control,* not lack of control. They actually speak to the opposite of who you are because you fight the thoughts that feel most unlike your nature. They may feel like strange urges, but they are not what you wish or want, even "unconsciously."

However, there are different kinds of thoughts and preoccupations that keep returning, but have a distinctly different feel to them. If you find yourself continually returning to the types of thoughts presented in the next few paragraphs, it is best that you speak about them with a mental health professional. There are just a few types of these thoughts, but you should know about them.

Invited Thoughts

Certain fantasies, thoughts, or images of self-destructive behavior can be actual urges to handle feelings or situations that seem intolerable. People sometimes call upon them in times of distress, and they seem soothing or comforting—like *escape plans* if things get too hard to bear. It is also the case that invited thoughts of revenge or outrage lead to actual plans to do harm to others. Here are some examples:

- *I want to cut myself because it makes me feel better after I do. At least it is visible, and I am in control of my pain. After I cut, I feel calmer or numb, and the mental pain goes away.*
- *I can always get drunk if I can't manage. So what; who cares?*
- *If she leaves me, I can always just jump off a building or shoot myself*

if I can't stand it. Then she will regret it.

- *I deserve to be treated better, so I will let the air out of his tires. Let him wonder who did it and why. It will be my little secret.*
- *If she says that one more time, I will hurt her.*

If thoughts or images become actual plans or actions that are destructive to others or self-harming, they do not qualify as unwanted intrusions, and treatment is recommended.

Real Suicidal Preoccupations

For people who are depressed and struggling, the feelings evoked by the thoughts are not *This is not me; I love my life, why would I even be thinking that?* but rather the feeling is a sincere wish to die. In harmless unwanted intrusive thoughts, it feels like this: *What if in a moment of craziness, I kill myself when I don't really want to?*

In contrast, in serious depression, it looks something like this:

- *I really deserve to die, or I actually want to die.*

- *This is hopeless; dying is my only option.*
- *My family will be better off without me. They will forgive me or will manage after a while.*
- *I can't stand living any more. I have to do something drastic.*

Although the thought repeats, the feeling of deserving to be dead is *totally* different from the fear that you might—despite your conscious intentions—do something harmful to yourself. These thoughts appear in the context of other symptoms of depression or bipolar illness, such as loss of appetite, trouble sleeping, a loss of the ability to feel pleasure, irritability, and feelings of worthlessness and hopelessness. The idea of being dead feels comforting or appropriate instead of frightening.

Real Pedophilia

People who are sexually attracted to and aroused by children are few and far between. Many have their own justifications that support what they are doing. Some resist their fantasies and activities seeking sex with children either because they know these activities are illegal and do not want to get caught or because they sincerely believe it to be wrong. However, they find themselves pulled toward risky illegal activities on the Internet—with child pornography or with real children, strangers, or family. The important distinction is to understand that pedophiles are looking for stimulation and arousal. They are seeking a sexual release.

On the other hand, people with unwanted intrusive thoughts involving the topic of pedophilia are shamefully and anxiously checking to see if they are perverted against their will, and—at the very same time—fervently hoping to prove that they are not. They are not looking for sexual stimulation; they are looking for reassurance that they are not the sort of person who is attracted to children.

If Perspective Is Entirely Lost

You might read this book and have no idea what we are saying or have no understanding of the points we are making. Or perhaps you think it is all nonsense. You might not be able to concentrate enough to think clearly. And this is not just a temporary feeling that lasts for a few minutes, a few hours, or a day or two, but something that seems pretty constant. In that case, reading this book is not going to provide answers.

Hopelessness

Sometimes a feeling of hopelessness is perceived as an actual fact. Hopeless feelings can happen even if the objective facts are that nothing at all is hopeless. In fact, hopeless feelings can happen in conditions that are easily treatable and situations that are easily fixed. The feeling of hopelessness can be sometimes made to seem more real by the struggle against it, as we have discussed in earlier chapters. However, hopeless feelings can lead to the false sense that there are no more options in your life, and so your life is over. This thought can repeat over and over. Here are some examples:

- I have lost everything. My boyfriend hates me, and I can never get him back. I am doing so badly in school that I will fail out. Even my friends see me as a loser and don't want to spend time with me. My life is over.
- There is no point is any of this. I am just a loser.

If you are truly unable to see beyond a feeling of hopelessness, it is time to seek professional help.

Agitation

Finally, there are times when racing thoughts can seem like intrusive thoughts. But racing thoughts are actually a symptom of agitation, which is associated with depression, bipolar disorder, or certain medical conditions. Racing thoughts tend to switch from topic to topic—they feel like you can't finish one before the next is there.

This agitation almost always goes along with other symptoms, including the inability to feel any pleasure in life (anhedonia) and early morning awakening (waking up with a "start" in the middle of the night, and then not being able to get back to sleep). People experience a significant change of appetites for food, sex, and ordinary daily activities. You might feel irritable, have a great difficulty with concentration, and feel utterly unable to relax. Your sense of humor might change. Because these feelings are so dramatic, agitation is often mistakenly called *extreme anxiety,* but in fact, it is a sign of depression or related conditions. It needs a different approach, very often medical in nature. It is highly treatable.

You may read this chapter and say, "Yes, that is me." And, if you do, the best help is from a professional, and not just a self-help book.

But you may wonder, debate, and worry about whether you fit in any of these categories, and that is normal for anyone suffering from unwanted intrusive thoughts. After all, doubt is the engine that fuels anxiety. In fact, it is likely that you do not fit into any of these categories, but you will still get great benefits from this book.

Acknowledgments

First, I would like to express my thanks to Marty Seif, who has been the driving force behind this book and the only person who has ever convinced me to write any book. Our process of nudging, affirming, cajoling, and arguing on Google Docs, on the phone, and in person has been a pleasure. His astute mind fuels my creativity and, at the same time, keeps me from being sloppy. My main teachers have been my patients, who have somehow found the courage to share their thoughts and feelings—even when they are disturbing, frightening, or embarrassing—and who have been willing to embark on many uncomfortable journeys of the mind with me. I am indebted as always to Steve Shearer, my codirector at the Anxiety and Stress Disorders Institute of Maryland, who has calmly and patiently managed so much more than his share of responsibilities while I have been writing and giving workshops. To my colleagues from whom I never stop learning—Reid Wilson, Carl Robbins,

David Carbonell, Jonathan Grayson, David Barlow, and so many others I have met through the Anxiety and Depression Association of America—I am always grateful. Thank you to Molly Winston, who created our graphics and who quietly tolerated confusing and conflicting revisions along the way. And I tip my hat to three amazing women no longer with us who had such a profound influence on my life and career: Jerilyn Ross, Alies Muskin, and Zelda Milstein.

—Sally Winston

Three years ago I wrote a single page on my website with the title "Intrusive Thoughts." It was listed under the "self-help" section and not at all easy to find. To my astonishment, that single page has been visited by almost half a million people over the past two years. People have written by the hundreds about their own situation, sometimes thanking me for the information I provide and sometimes asking how to find additional help. I became educated about the need for more help. And so this book was born.

I start by expressing my appreciation to Sally Winston, my coauthor. Sally has been my friend and colleague for many years, and co-writing this book with her has been a delightful task as we discussed, disputed, and edited each other's words and ideas. I am fortunate that she has granted me access to her steady, thoughtful, inquisitive, and knowledgeable mind. Next, it is almost *de rigeur* to thank one's clients at this point, but this book would never have been conceived without the input of so many of you who suffer from UITs. I thank Ron

Doctor for our long term friendship and Reid Wilson for openly sharing his findings on how to help people understand the riddle of anxiety. Finally, I am indebted to those no longer with us who taught me that anxiety need not restrict my life: Manny Zane, Herb Fensterheim, Jerilyn Ross, Sabe Basescu, Isadore From.

—Martin Seif

APPENDIX

A Recipe for Unwanted Intrusive Thoughts (What Not to Do)

It isn't easy to create an unwanted intrusive thought. It takes vigilance, effort, and a relentless desire to think the right thoughts. Amazingly, almost all the energy you pour into making sure that your thought doesn't get stuck goes right into ensuring that it happens. What is interesting, however, is that with the right ingredients, anyone can create one. You will notice as you read this recipe that it illustrates all the concepts we have introduced. So let's look closely and see how your best intentions go so wrong!

A Recipe for Creating an Unwanted Intrusive Thought

Time required: Varies from less than one day to several weeks

Difficulty: Three of five stars

Effort: Five of five stars

Ingredients

- one (or more) myths about thoughts (see chapter 3)
- awareness of the passing intrusive thoughts, which everyone has
- vigilance to make sure you don't have those thoughts
- a desire to fight any thought that is at odds with your belief about yourself
- one amygdala (the alarm part of the brain, which everyone has)
- being bluffed by the altered state of awareness called "anxious thinking"
- willingness to struggle to keep a sticky thought from getting more stuck
- a demand for certainty when none is possible
- the belief that surrendering the struggle is losing the fight

- attempts to avoid, distract, push away, and argue with your stuck thought
- feeling guilty about having the thought, even after it is over, and then asking others for forgiveness or confirmation of your value and goodness as a person
- and, finally, reassurance (from yourself or others) that you would never do anything like your thought
- o p t i o n a l   a d d i t i o n a l ingredients—anxiety (these are starter ingredients):
    - fatigue, hunger, or a hangover
    - family or personal history of anxiety

Directions

Choose one or more myths from chapter 3. Our personal favorites are the myth that your thoughts are under your control and the myth that your thoughts speak to your character or underlying intentions. When you combine them together, you have a solid basis for creating some unwanted intrusive thoughts. However, any combination of myths can yield an excellent unwanted intrusive thought.

The next part is probably the easiest and requires very little effort. Just go about living your life, feeling everyday feelings, and having everyday thoughts. Enjoy this part, because it won't go on for all that long. Here is why.

Worried Voice: It's not good to have me in the kitchen. I could pick up a knife and stab you!

False Comfort: You are scaring me, Worried Voice. Do you want me to lock the drawers and hide the knives?

Worried Voice: Well, it would make me feel better, but this rolling pin—I could just bash you in the head with it!

False Comfort: Maybe I should get out of your way? Am I far enough from you? We could just not cook today.

Wise Mind: What's all this fuss about? Thoughts are thoughts. They are bluffing you. Get on with the recipe, knives and all. I'm hungry.

Soon, in the course of living your life, you will have a passing intrusive thought. We know this will happen because everyone has passing intrusive thoughts. This just happens; it is not under your control.

Now is the time to add ingredients. This part is up to you, but don't worry. *Anyone* using this recipe will be able to produce an unwanted intrusive thought. You have to latch on to this thought. You have to notice it and see if this thought can possibly mean something bad about your character or underlying intentions. (We are referring to the two myths mentioned above.)

Here is where your mental effort and your belief system start to work together. If this *passing* thought can mean something about you and if you honestly believe that the *content* of your thought doesn't fit with your sense of the sort of person you are, then you will begin to wonder and doubt yourself. And you will enter a very uncomfortable zone of uncertainty. Psychologists call this a form of "cognitive dissonance," where your thoughts and your feelings seem uncomfortably different.

And if that possibility exists (and of course it is impossible to absolutely prove that it doesn't), you then have to make sure that the thought doesn't come back again. Because if it intrudes again, then it reinforces that there is something bad about your character or intentions. And you believe with all your heart that this is *not* true. So those thoughts better stay away, and it feels as if your job is to make sure that happens.

For this next step, the struggle starts in earnest. You are fighting the thoughts, but they continue to return. You are encountering the ironic effect: the more you try to keep these thoughts from your mind, the more they intrude. The more they intrude, the more frustrated and anxious you become. You start to wonder if perhaps you aren't as good a person as you had believed. After all, how could a good person have such a twisted mind? Remember, if you are going to be successful at creating a stuck intrusive thought, you have to react to an ordinary passing thought with distress, alarm, and upset. Otherwise it will just pass, you will forget it or laugh about it, and the recipe will be ruined.

Here are a variety of kitchen hints you may use to ensure that the thoughts will become stuck, repetitive, and distressing. Some of them are probably already familiar to you.

- Try hard to think of an explanation for these thoughts.
- Use your *rational* mind to counteract the product of your *irrational* mind.
- Think of how much better things would be *if only* you hadn't done something, gone someplace, watched some TV show, or whatever that seemed to trigger the thought.
- Imagine how awful you would feel or what terrible things would happen, if you *actually acted* on your intrusive thought.
- Be stern with yourself as a way to make sure you keep disciplined and don't let the thought creep in. Criticize yourself strongly if they do.
- Think about how much easier it would be if you only could be

certain that you would never act on your awful thought!

As you work even harder, you experience the fact that your effort appears to work backward. Your energy seems to give power to the thought, and, in contrast, you begin to feel much less powerful, almost as if there were a strong impulse forcing you to act against your will. Your brain and body are in alarm mode, and you are primed for danger.

You can be sure you are in alarm mode by noticing the enormous feeling of whoosh that starts low down in your belly and rushes up to your head. That whoosh is the best indication that you are correctly following directions to this point. If there is no whoosh of distress, pick another passing thought or work harder at fighting or being appalled by it.

You now enter the altered state of awareness that we call anxious thinking. Anxious thinking is what happens to everyone when the alarm system in their brain goes off. Think of this as your adrenaline surge. The part of your brain that triggers this alarm—the amygdala—starts responding with its fight, flight, or freeze response. (This reaction has a number of names, including, "stress reaction" and "danger reaction.")

The perceptual changes that are part of anxious thinking contribute to the increasing belief that the intrusive thoughts mean more than ordinary thoughts. They start to feel like impulses that need to be resisted.

At this point, your body is in alarm mode, and you are experiencing a range of physical sensations indicating what psychologists call "high autonomic arousal." In regular words, it means that your entire nervous system is primed for danger, and you are doing whatever you can to keep yourself safe. You are at a critical point in the recipe, so don't even think of stopping! Imagine that you are making a soufflé. There is a point in every soufflé recipe when you have to *go with your feelings* so the soufflé doesn't fall, yet doesn't overbake. In a similar manner, it is just as important to the success of this recipe that you *go with your feelings, whether they are fear, disgust, shame, or shock* and listen to what your alarm system is telling you. You must allow yourself to believe that the alarm sounded by your amygdala and felt in your body is a true alarm—a message of warning not to be ignored. If you don't and if you start thinking it might be silly or is overreacting or a false alarm, it will result in a failed attempt. So be sure to take your amygdala seriously.

You can now congratulate yourself. Merely by following these simple directions, you have created an unwanted intrusive thought from a completely ordinary passing thought. And, if you want, you are ready to sit down at the table and serve your recipe to others.

But wait! There's more!

For added touches that ensure that your unwanted intrusive thought won't fade away prior to getting maximum suffering, you can include the following:

- Feel guilty and ask others for forgiveness.
- Explain that you are not the type of person who wants to do the things in your intrusion. Ask for

reassurance that you would *never* do something like that.

- Check with others to determine if you seem weird or odd, and whether your behavior caused them discomfort.
- Condiments might include a few sprigs of shame and a dollop of anger.

To ensure misery and distress, repeat this recipe as often as possible. Daily practice is preferable, although some people need to start slow with only the occasional effort and pick up speed and frequency over time. Once you are practiced at this recipe, you eventually find it possible to easily ruin a good day. Merely follow the steps above, which become quite automatic.

Now that you know how unwanted intrusive thoughts are created, refer back to chapter 6 to remind yourself why you feel so frustrated.

Bibliography

Baer, L. 2001. *Imp of the Mind.* New York: Penguin.

Borkovec, T.D., Robinson, E., Pruzinsky, T., and Depree, J.A. 1983. "Preliminary Exploration of Worry: Some Characteristics and Processes." *Behaviour Research and Therapy* 21(1): 9–16.

Brewin, C.R., Gregory, J.D., Lipton, M., and Burgess, N. 2010. "Intrusive Images in Psychological Disorders: Characteristics, Neural Mechanisms, and Treatment Implications." *Psychological Review* 117(1): 210–32.

Carbonell, D. 2016. *The Worry Trick: How Your Brain Tricks You into Expecting the Worst and What You Can Do About It.* Oakland, CA: New Harbinger Publications.

Craske, M.G., K. Kircanski, M. Zelikowsky, J. Mystkowski, J. Chowdhury, and A. Baker. January

2008. "Optimizing Inhibitory Learning During Exposure Therapy." *Behaviour Research and Therapy* 46(1): 5–27.

Foa, E.B., and Kozak, M.J. 1986. "Emotional Processing of Fear: Exposure to Corrective Information." *Psychological Bulletin* 99(1): 20.

Forsythe, J. and G.H. Eifert. 2007. *The Mindfulness and Acceptance Workbook for Anxiety.* Oakland, CA: New Harbinger Publications.

Grayson, J. 2003. *Freedom from Obsessive Compulsive Disorder.* New York: Berkley Books.

Hershfield, J., T. Corboy, and J. Claiborn. 2013. *The Mindfulness Workbook for OCD.* Oakland, CA: New Harbinger Publications.

Leahy, R. 2005. *The Worry Cure.* New York: Three Rivers Press.

LeDoux, J. 1998. *The Emotional Brain: The Mysterious Underpinnings of*

Emotional Life. New York: Simon and Schuster.

Pittman, C.M. and E.M. Karle. 2015. *Rewire Your Anxious Brain: How to Use the Neuroscience of Fear to End Anxiety, Panic, and Worry.* Oakland, CA: New Harbinger Publications.

Rachman, S. 1993. "Obsessions, Responsibility and Guilt." *Behaviour Research and Therapy* 31(2): 149–154.

Salkovskis, P.M. 1985. "Obsessional-Compulsive Problems: A Cognitive-Behavioural Analysis." *Behaviour Research and Therapy* 23(5): 571–83.

Stoddard, J.A., N. Afari, and S.C. Hayes. 2014. *The Big Book of ACT Metaphors.* Oakland, CA: New Harbinger Publications.

Teresa, M. 2009. *Come Be My Light.* New York: Random House.

Weekes, C. 1969. *Hope and Help for Your Nerves.* New York: Hawthorne Books.

Wegner, D.M. 1994. "Ironic Processes of Mental Control." *Psychological Review* 1: 34–52.

Sally M. Winston, PsyD, founded and codirects the Anxiety and Stress Disorders Institute of Maryland in Towson, MD. She served as the first chair of the Clinical Advisory Board of the Anxiety and Depression Association of America (ADAA), and received their prestigious Jerilyn Ross Clinician Advocate Award. She is a master clinician who has given sought-after workshops for therapists for decades. She is coauthor of *What Every Therapist Needs to Know About Anxiety Disorders.*

Martin N. Seif, PhD, cofounded the Anxiety and Depression Association of America, and was a member of its board of directors from 1977 through 1991. Seif is associate director of The Anxiety and Phobia Treatment Center at White Plains Hospital, a faculty member of NewYork-Presbyterian Hospital, and is board certified in cognitive behavioral psychology from the American Board of Professional Psychology. He maintains a private practice in New York, NY, and Greenwich, CT, and is coauthor of *What Every Therapist Needs to Know About Anxiety Disorders.*

MORE BOOKS *from*
NEW HARBINGER PUBLICATIONS

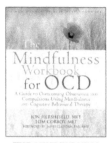

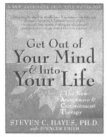

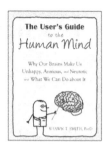

THE MINDFULNESS WORKBOOK FOR OCD

A Guide to Overcoming Obsessions & Compulsions Using Mindfulness & Cognitive Behavioral Therapy

GET OUT OF YOUR MIND & INTO YOUR LIFE

The New Acceptance & Commitment Therapy

THE USER'S GUIDE TO THE HUMAN MIND

Why Our Brains Make Us Unhappy, Anxious & Neurotic & What We Can Do about It

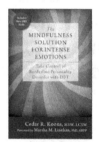

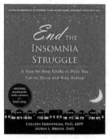

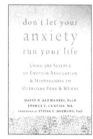

THE MINDFULNESS SOLUTION FOR INTENSE EMOTIONS

Take Control of Borderline Personality Disorder with DBT

END THE INSOMNIA STRUGGLE

A Step-by-Step Guide to Help You Get to Sleep & Stay Asleep

DON'T LET YOUR ANXIETY RUN YOUR LIFE

Using the Science of Emotion Regulation & Mindfulness to Overcome Fear & Worry

 newharbingerpublications
1-800-748-6273 / newharbinger.com

(VISA, MC, AMEX / prices subject to change without notice)

Follow Us 🅵 🆇 🄾 🅿 Don't miss out on new books in the subjects that interest you.
Sign up for our **Book Alerts** at **newharbinger.com/bookalerts**

ARE YOU SEEKING A CBT THERAPIST?

The Association for Behavioral & Cognitive Therapies (ABCT) Find-a-Therapist service offers a list of therapists schooled in CBT techniques. Therapists listed are licensed professionals who have met the membership requirements of ABCT and who have chosen to appear in the directory.

Please visit www.abct.org and click on *Find a Therapist*.

Back Cover Material

It's not what you think!

If you suffer from frightening, obsessive, or disturbing thoughts, you know all too well how they can intrude on your life. You may even worry what these thoughts mean about you. Do they make you a bad person? No! You aren't bad—or crazy. These upsetting thoughts that enter your mind unbidden are called *unwanted intrusive thoughts,* and many rational and good people have them. Fortunately, there are proven-effective techniques you can use now to move past these thoughts and reclaim your life.

This powerful guide offers an evidence-based cognitive behavioral therapy (CBT) approach to help you get unstuck from distressing thoughts; overcome feelings of guilt, shame, and loneliness that can accompany these thoughts; and reduce your overall anxiety. You'll learn about the different types of unwanted thoughts, *why* these thoughts keep getting stuck, and ways to break out of this vicious cycle. Finally, you'll discover how changes in attitude and beliefs can help you move beyond your thoughts so you can focus on the things that really matter.

"Sally Winston and Martin Seif—two of the brightest minds in our field—deliver a simple yet powerful two-step process for change."
—REID WILSON, PHD, author of *Stopping the Noise in Your Heade*

***

SALLY M. WINSTON, PSYD, founded and codirects the Anxiety and Stress Disorders Institute of Maryland. She is coauthor, with Martin N. Seif, of *What Every Therapist Needs to Know About Anxiety Disorders.*

MARTIN N. SEIF, PHD, cofounded the Anxiety and Depression Association of America. He maintains a private practice in New York, NY, and Greenwich, CT.